DOUBLE EXPOSURE

GAME CHANGERS

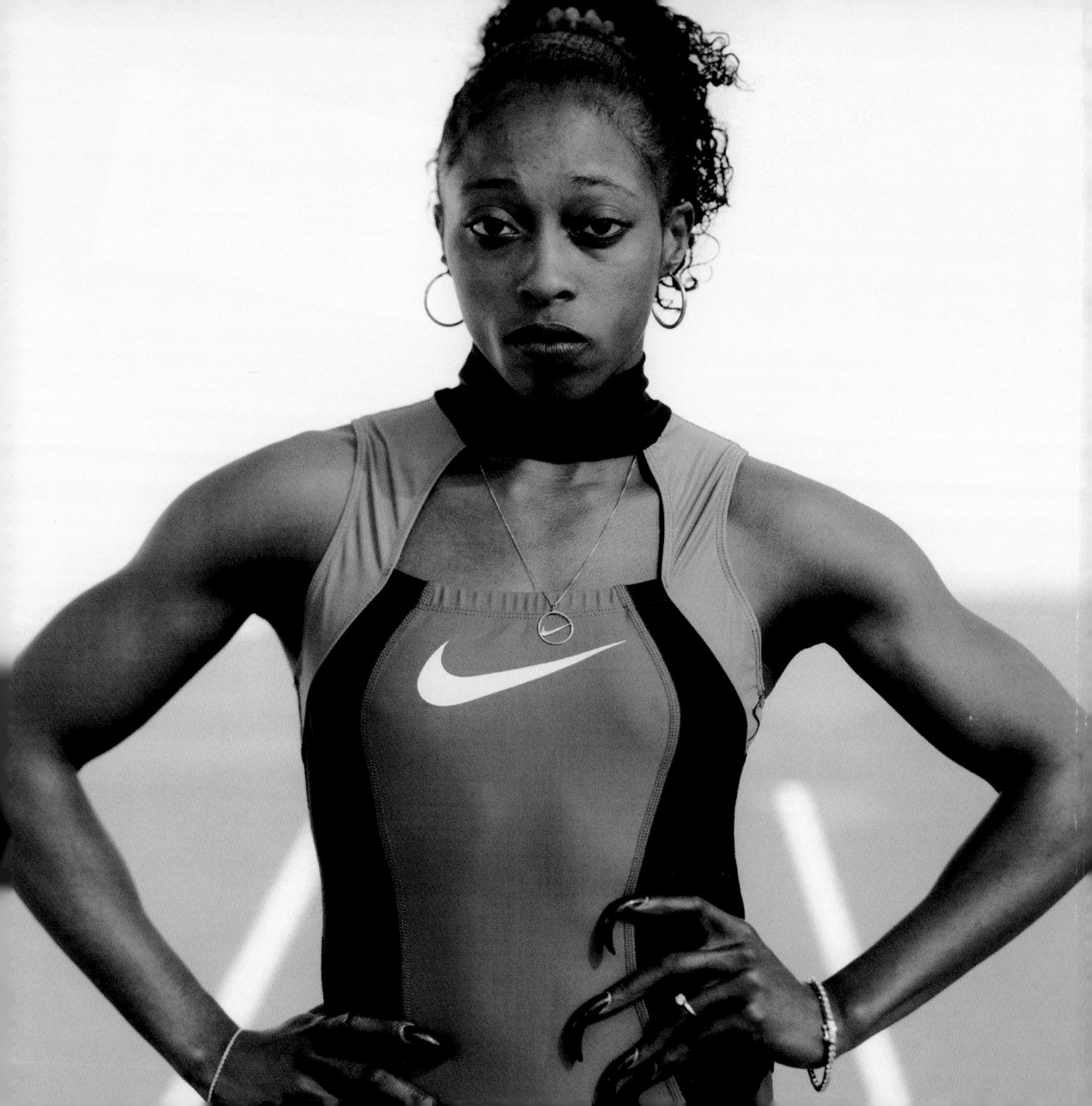

DOUBLE EXPOSURE

GAME CHANGERS

Sports Photographs from the National Museum of African American History and Culture

NATIONAL MUSEUM *of* AFRICAN AMERICAN HISTORY & CULTURE

Earl W. and Amanda Stafford
Center for African American Media Arts

GILES

National Museum of African American History and Culture
Smithsonian Institution, Washington, D.C., in association with D Giles Limited

For the National Museum of African American History and Culture
Series Editors: Laura Coyle and Michèle Gates Moresi

Project Coordinator: Douglas Remley

Publication Committee: Laura Coyle, Shi Evans, Michèle Gates Moresi, Loren E. Miller, Douglas Remley, Melanie Taylor, Damion Thomas, and David K. Wiggins

Photograph Conservator: Mirasol Estrada

This project is supported by NMAAHC Sports Leadership Council: The Brooklyn Nets & New York Liberty Foundation; LA Clippers Foundation; Robert K. Kraft Family, The New England Patriots Charitable Foundation; San Antonio Spurs; Washington Commanders

For D Giles Limited
Copyedited and proofread by Jodi Simpson
Designed by Alfonso Iacurci
Produced by GILES, an imprint of D Giles Limited
Printed and bound in Italy

MIX
Paper | Supporting responsible forestry
FSC® C015829
www.fsc.org

First published in 2024 by GILES
An imprint of D Giles Limited
66 High Street
Lewes
BN7 1XG
gilesltd.com

ISBN: 978-1-913875-76-3

All measurements are in inches and centimeters; height precedes width precedes depth.

Photograph titles: Where a photographer has designated a title for his/her photograph, this title is shown in italics. All other titles are descriptive and are not italicized.

Front cover: Doug Williams, Tampa Bay Buccaneers vs. Green Bay Packers, Green Bay, Wisconsin, October 29, 1978 (detail), Vandell Cobb

Back cover: *Connie Morgan, Martin Stadium, Memphis, TN*, ca. 1954 (detail), Ernest C. Withers

Frontispiece: *Gail Devers, Los Angeles, California*, 1996 (detail), Walter Iooss Jr.

Foreword

The Black athlete has long served as a symbol of excellence, a figure of change, and an image of the otherwise impossible. We soar when they do; we root for them even as we doubt; we win even when they lose, as long as the attempt proves as noble as the victory.

Yet when I look through the photos found in *Game Changers*, all from the growing, generative collection at the National Museum of African American History and Culture, I think less of the sports they feature than I do of poetry. Granted, I often am thinking of poetry—especially having written a number of poems about the many sports figures who have inspired me, from Jack Johnson, Arthur Ashe, and Wilma Rudolph to Muhammad Ali, Henry "Hank" Aaron, and the Harlem Globetrotters. But Black athletes themselves provide a sense of image and line, memory and music and movement also found in poetry. As poetry makes its connections, performs its praise, so too do these photographs of Black figures in the serious play found in sports.

What these photographs aren't is silent. This book is the first in the *Double Exposure* series to include photographs from the Johnson Publishing Company Archive, co-owned by the Museum and the Getty Research Institute and made up of more than four million negatives, images, and audio visual media. More than twenty of the photographs in this book, spanning almost forty years, come from the Johnson Publishing Company collection, remarkable for its

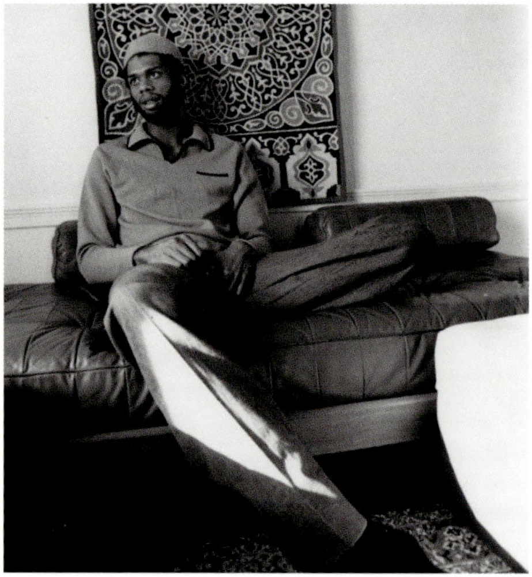

Kareem Abdul-Jabbar at home, Milwaukee, Wisconsin, 1975 (detail)
Ozier Muhammad

ability to get inside athletes' homes and experiences, documenting ordinary moments in often extraordinary lives. While no one dares to speak for these athletes—certainly Muhammad Ali and the Williams sisters can speak for themselves—the photographs, often made by Black photographers, do directly communicate with the viewer. Pictures such as Kareem Abdul-Jabbar in his home's sacred prayer space reveal an essential side of athletes that goes well beyond the court.

Just as powerful as the famed athletes featured here are those unknown to us but bold and embodied nonetheless. Whether a boyish boxer or woman archer from the 1940s, or cheerleaders, coaches, women and men's basketball players, and track stars from Historically Black Colleges and Universities, who have long represented the vanguard of

Black achievement on the field and off, these beloved amateurs inspire us to leap beyond our current moment.

We are grateful for the Sports Leadership Council, which funded this project, representing a dedicated group of organizations, teams, and individuals whose financial support fuels initiatives that use the lens of the African American sports experience to address the ongoing legacies of slavery, stimulate constructive dialogues about race, and promote a spirit of reconciliation and healing. Another initiative supporting this volume is the Earl W. and Amanda Stafford Center for African American Media Arts (CAAMA), a physical and virtual resource within NMAAHC that exemplifies the Museum's commitment to preserving African American history and culture.

This ninth volume in the *Double Exposure* series is realized thanks to those who have collaborated on this important book. Special acknowledgement goes to the Publication Team: Laura Coyle, Assistant Director for Cataloging and Digitization; Shi Evans, Sports Researcher and Project Assistant; Michèle Gates Moresi, Assistant Director for Collections, who serves with Laura as co-editor of this series; Loren E. Miller, Museum Specialist; Douglas Remley, Rights and Publications Manager and Project Coordinator for the series; Melanie Taylor, Curatorial Assistant; and Damion Thomas, Curator of Sports. I'd like to extend a special thanks to David K. Wiggins, Professor Emeritus of Sport Studies at George Mason University, whose foremost knowledge of the role and impact of African Americans on American sports has been vital to the creation and development of this publication. A word of thanks also goes to Mirasol Estrada, Photographs Conservator, for preparing many of these photographs for inclusion in the book, while ongoing support and encouragement from the Museum's Deputy Director, Michelle D. Commander, has been invaluable to the continuation of the series.

We are also fortunate to have the pleasure of co-publishing with D Giles Limited. The team would like particularly to thank Dan Giles, Managing Director; Alfonso Iacurci, Designer; Allison McCormick, Editorial Director; Louise Ramsay, Production Director; Jodi Simpson, copy editor and proofreader; and Liz Japes, Sales and Marketing Manager. Finally, I would like to thank the Museum's Digitization Team for researching, cataloging, and digitizing the images included in this volume.

As the Museum's large and revelatory collection of sports artifacts demonstrates, the athletes here sought to level the playing field. Their efforts and their victories are as much a form of activism as any other—offering poetry, prayer, and a real sense of possibility.

Kevin Young
Andrew W. Mellon Director

Playing to Win

Damion Thomas, Curator of Sports
David K. Wiggins, Professor Emeritus of Sport Studies

As historians who have been educated to write extended academic books, we have found it challenging and rewarding to tell the story of the African American experience in sport through a careful selection of about sixty images from the roughly 2,200 sports-related photographs within the Museum's collection. As you might expect, we had to make some difficult choices. For example, while African American sports history did not begin in 1910—in fact, there were a select number of African American athletes who distinguished themselves in their respective sports at all levels of competition prior to this time—we chose to begin our book with the fight featuring Jack Johnson and Jim Jeffries because this moment encapsulates our core message: sports matter, and they matter far beyond the playing field. This sports moment, perhaps more significantly than any other sporting event before it, illustrates how deeply sports are intertwined with notions of race and equal access to opportunity.

When selecting these images, we had to make some tough decisions: Should the book present the Black body in motion? Should we choose images that reflect the most iconic moments in sports history? Should we focus on recreational sports or highly competitive amateur and professional teams and players? Should this book concentrate on social justice? Wrestling with these questions helped guide our work. Ultimately, we chose to incorporate images that speak to all these questions. Convinced that such an approach is appropriate, our aim is not to tell sports history, but rather to engage the depth, beauty, and challenges of African American history through the lens of sport photography.

This collection of images is divided into four sections that capture the fight for access, opportunity, advancement, and excellence. Some images might be dated outside of the section's timeframe, but they speak to that era's significance.

Survival and Community Building: 1900–1945

Although negatively impacted by two world

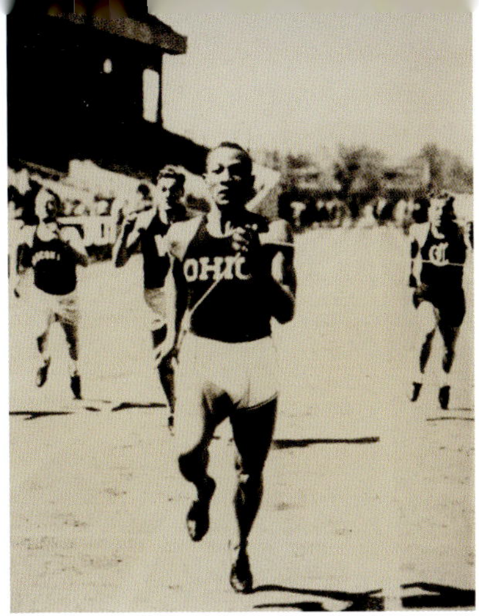

Jesse Owens crossing the finish line, ca. 1935
Keystone

wars, the Great Depression, continued racial segregation, and a host of other constraints, the images in this section show that African Americans carved out for themselves a vibrant yet diverse sporting culture that was essential to their survival and community building. For African Americans, Jack Johnson's 1910 victory over Jim Jeffries (see p. 18) revealed how sports could be used to contradict widespread racist ideas. This period is also noteworthy for the number of notable African American athletes, many of them originally from the South, who would distinguish themselves and serve as important examples of achievement and symbols of possibility. They carved out successful careers in intercollegiate sports at predominantly white colleges that accepted Black students, including 1936 Olympic stars Jesse Owens and Ralph Metcalfe (see p. 25).

Equally important, because of persistent racially discriminatory practices, this period saw the establishment of vibrant and highly competitive athletic programs at Historically Black Colleges and Universities (HBCUs), such as Samuel Huston College and Tuskegee Institute (see pp. 22 and 23). These separate or "parallel" teams, leagues, and organizations created behind the walls of segregation were all important for allowing individuals to satisfy their competitive urges, but also crucial in illuminating racial pride, providing opportunities to exercise agency, and exhibiting business acumen and organizational skills. Nowhere was this more evident than in the success of the New York Rens (see p. 24), the first Black-owned professional basketball team, which reflects African Americans' efforts to use sports as a form of racial uplift.

Struggle and Breakthrough: 1945–1968

The signing of Jackie Robinson to a contract with the Brooklyn Dodgers organization on October 23, 1945, was a monumental event in race relations specifically and American history more generally. One of the unintended consequences of the integration of Major League Baseball was the decline of the Negro Leagues, which had been the crown jewel of the "parallel" sports. Black fans followed the Negro Leagues closely, and sportswriters from Black weeklies recounted the exploits of players whose names still resonate today,

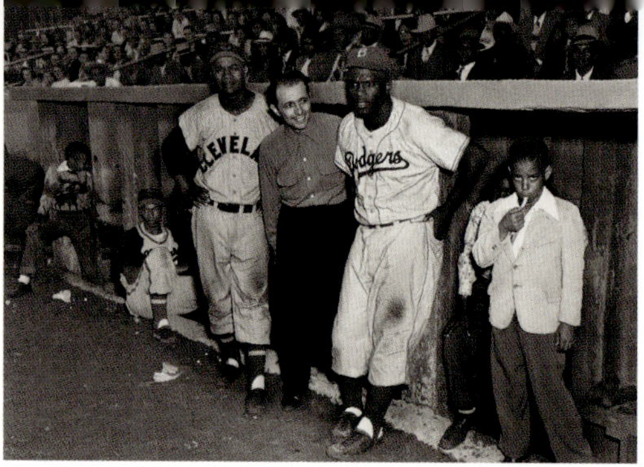

Ernie Banks, Larry Doby, Matty Brescia, Jackie Robinson, Martin Stadium, Memphis, TN, 1953
Ernest C. Withers

even with the most casual observers of the game. Despite their decline, the festive atmosphere typified by Martin Stadium (see pp. 30, 31, and 37), daring base running, and innovative aspects of the Negro Leagues were carried to the Major Leagues by African American fans and leading players like Willie Mays and Hank Aaron.

With the notable exceptions of Jackie Robinson and Bill Russell, most of the athletes involved in the initial wave of African American athletes who integrated sports were not closely involved in the civil rights struggle, nor did they speak out on larger racial issues. Athletes such as Willie Mays, Wilt Chamberlain, Larry Doby, Althea Gibson, and Floyd Patterson preferred to let their athletic accomplishments speak as refutations of dominant racist beliefs. That began to change in the 1960s, however, when a select number of African American athletes were inspired by Dr. Martin Luther King Jr., Malcolm X, and other leaders of the Civil Rights Movement. Encouraged by the well-orchestrated freedom rides, sit-ins, and voter registration drives, athletes shed their traditionally more conservative approach to racial matters and turned their attention to the racial inequality in sports.

Disruption and Acceptance: 1968–1980

As the photographs in this section reveal, activist athletes reminded people that although the sports world had made important strides, crucial battles remained, including the unequal salaries paid to African American athletes relative to their white counterparts; the stacking of African American athletes in non-leadership positions on the playing field; the underrepresentation of African American athletes in many so-called country-club sports; and the lack of African American head coaches, managers, and upper-level administrators at all levels of sports. The latter topic remains extraordinarily controversial, and rightfully so due to the underrepresentation of African Americans in leadership positions in sports.

What is striking about this era is that many of the protests waged had international implications: Arthur Ashe's stance against the apartheid system in South Africa; Lew Alcindor's decision to take the Arabic name Kareem Abdul-Jabbar; and Muhammad Ali's triumphant return to the ring after being barred from boxing for refusing induction into the military during the Vietnam War (see p. 50). Most notable was the proposed boycott of the 1968 Mexico City Olympic Games by African American athletes orchestrated by Harry Edwards, a sociology professor at San Jose State College. The boycott never took place. Instead, African American athletes chose various forms of protest to make the struggle for human rights visible around the world. The most famous of these was the black-gloved protest by Tommie Smith and John Carlos while on the victory stand following their first and third place finishes in the 200-meter race.

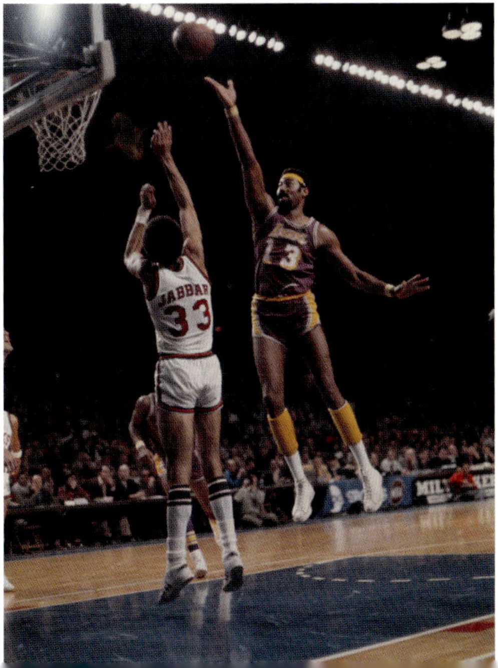

Wilt Chamberlain and Kareem Abdul-Jabbar, 1972
Theodore Williams

Innovation and Dominance: 1980–Today

African Americans have made significant progress in the world of sports in the last several decades, both in the United States and on the world stage. They have forged their way into sports that have traditionally been closed off to them. In increasing numbers, African Americans are now competing more often in leadership playing positions such as quarterback in football. Furthermore, they now claim a larger number of head coaching, managerial, and upper-level administrative positions; become owners of professional sports franchises; earn enormous salaries and endorsement deals; and continue to bring honor and prestige to the United States via their exploits through achievements in sports at the international level of competition.

Basketball is the sport in which African Americans have become most prominent, and with which they have become closely identified. Legendary players such as Michael Jordan, Kobe Bryant, and Magic Johnson revolutionized the sport and contributed to its global popularity. Kareem Abdul-Jabbar and LeBron James have effectively used their platform to promote social justice causes.

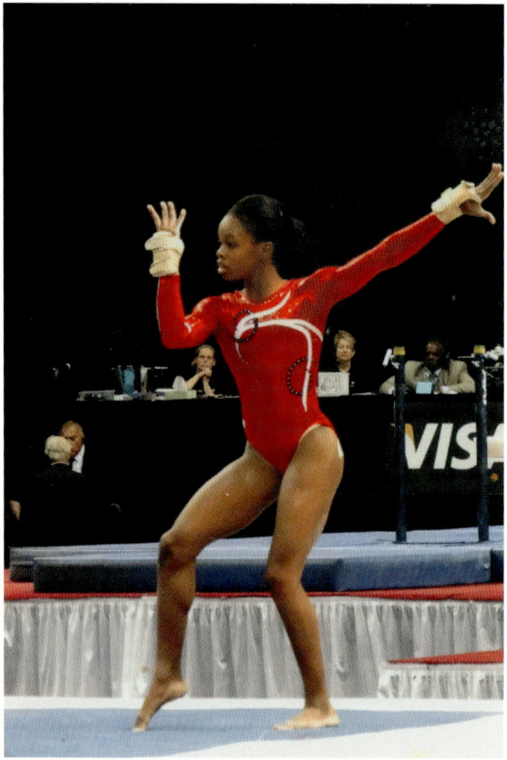

Gabby Douglas during the
U.S. National Gymnastics
Championships, August 2011
Unidentified photographer

African American women athletes—including Venus Williams, Gabby Douglas, Gail Devers, and Briana Scurry—have increasingly distinguished themselves in sports ranging from tennis and gymnastics to basketball and track and field. They recognized that vigorous competitive sports could contribute positively to their overall growth and development, and like their male counterparts they are active participants in the struggle for human rights.

One event during this period that garnered an inordinate amount of publicity and controversy was Colin Kaepernick's decision to take a knee during the National Anthem at National Football League games in protest of police brutality and the unjustified killing of Black men and women (see p. 81). Occurring in the midst of the Black Lives Matter movement, Kaepernick incurred the wrath of millions of Americans for his silent gesture but lasting praise from many others for his brave decision to disrupt what has been called the "sacred institution of sports" to make a point about persistent inequality and racially discriminatory practices in the United States. Importantly, Kaepernick's protests brought immediate comparisons with Tommie Smith's and John Carlos's actions on the victory stand in Mexico City almost fifty years earlier. Despite the advancements during this era, much still needs to be done regarding the quest for equal rights.

Working on this book has extended our appreciation of photography as a medium to convey the crucially important space that sports hold in the African American fight for greater rights, freedoms, and acceptance of African American cultural contributions. We hope that you find similar value in these pages.

Run, Jab, Float

Domonique Foxworth
Retired NFL Cornerback and Former President of the NFL Players Association

One image among the dozens of sports photos featured in this book acts as a proxy for the group. Its kineticism in black and white is emblematic of the elements of art, spectacle, and physical singularity that reliably mark Black athletic grace. The photo was taken in the Bronzeville neighborhood of 1940s Chicago, but it loses its time stamp when you focus on the girl jumping to the rhythm of the Double Dutch ropes. As the ropes strike the snow-covered pavement, she's confident and powerful while suspended in a kind of limbo. The ropes themselves act as a kind of whirring eye with the girl centered inside. The eye invites the viewer to appreciate the action—or, more specifically, the dozens of high-level decisions and acrobatic actions that so often typify Black

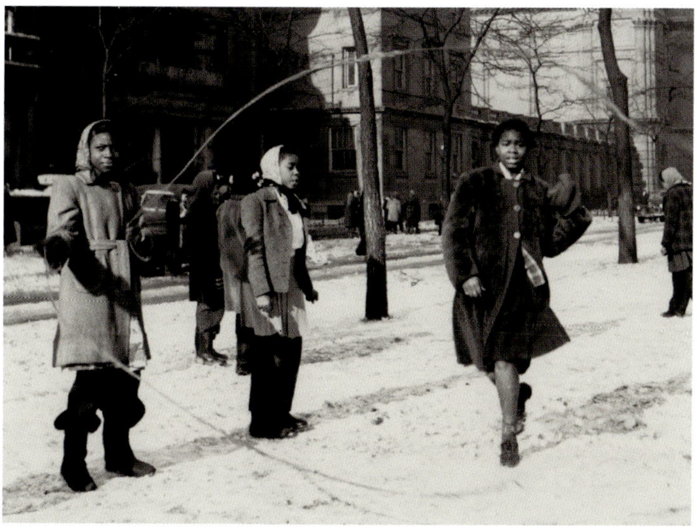

Double Dutch, Chicago, 1946–48; printed later
From the series The Way of Life of the Northern Negro
Wayne F. Miller

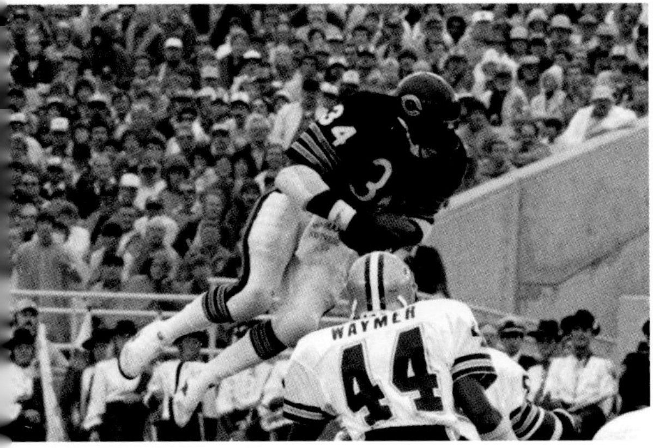

Walter Payton, Chicago Bears
vs. New Orleans Saints, Chicago,
Illinois, September 2, 1984 (detail)
Vandell Cobb

people at play. However, metaphorically, we know this is not just play; there's more at stake because, in Double Dutch as in life, Black people can't afford a misstep. So, they learn to run, jab, float.

The image reminds me of being "Air-aware," as Michael Jordan was in the 1989 NBA Slam Dunk Contest (see p. 67), gliding to the basket with a grace and physicality that turns even opponents into admirers and fans. It's an athletic feat punctuating the changes he made to the game itself, the world's perception of the NBA, and the soaring capacity of the human body. Seemingly, if only for a wisp of a moment, he is a Black man in control of all the forces in the world that act against us. For a second, to rise or fall is simply a choice.

We see similar elements of the photo of the girl jumping rope in the images of Walter Payton and Venus Williams. Payton, the Hall of Fame running back, created an on-field running style so exceptional it earned him the nickname "Sweetness." It sounds incongruent with the brutality of the NFL until you see the photo of him soaring over the trenches. "Sweetness" somehow perfectly describes both the sudden speed and power of that rugged running back and the precision of that young girl inside those Double Dutch ropes. Additionally a glow radiates from an eleven-year-old Venus Ebony Starr Williams who is framed by limitless sky. Her features sparkle with youth and possibility, and she shines down from above like a guiding star that the tennis world would have no choice but to follow. Her wide eyes hint at the confidence—and the resilience—she will need as she grows into center court.

How you interpret a photo tells you a lot about what's happening in the world of that picture, but it's also about what is happening in your own world. Looking at these photographs, I wanted to see the purity of athletes in their lanes of competition. I wanted to see these photos as a celebration of Blackness—untainted by their circumstances, irrespective of where or how they were taken. But I cannot see the beauty of Black athletes without thinking of the society in which they perform.

The photo of Lee Elder, at the 1975 Master's Tournament in Augusta (see p. 61), finds the pro golfer wrapped in

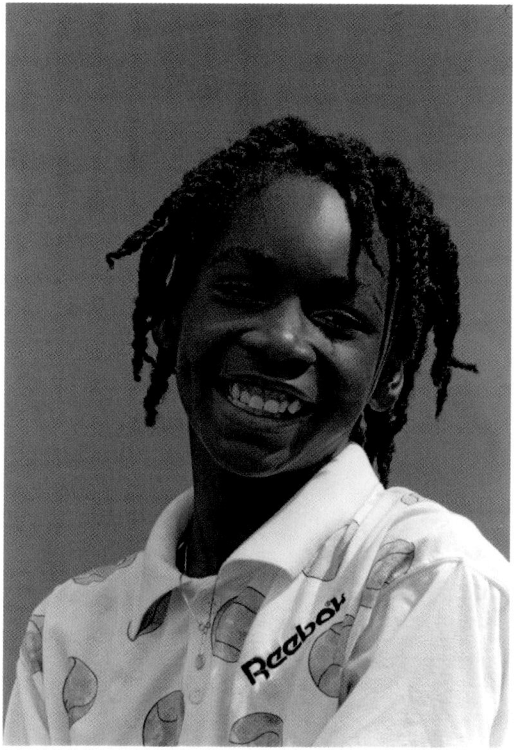

Venus, 1991
Roderick J. Lyons

attention-grabbing bright red from head to toe—as if the first Black person ever invited to play at Augusta would need any help standing out. His left hand rests on his hip, while his right hand helps balance his weight on the club at his side. The story in his stance, surveying the course, suggests an archetype that Black people know at a glance: the one who holds the space and paves the way and demands to be seen and heard.

This dynamic is also present in a 1915 fight photo (see p. 16) in which heavyweight champion Jack Johnson appears to be winning against white opponent Jess Willard in a bout slated to go forty-five rounds. He's punching Willard, who falls back to defend himself. Johnson dominates, but the image of him striking a white man sets off my alarms. The fight took place during a period called the nadir for African Americans because of white supremacist violence, disenfranchisement, and discrimination. Historically, African Americans found themselves on the wrong side of every sanctioned ass whooping, in a country still programmed against our winning, always primed for white vengeance.

In 1910, Johnson's victory in the ring against white opponent James J. Jeffries (see p. 18) triggered race riots across the United States, and in 1912, he was the victim of a racially motivated arrest and fled the United States to avoid prison. In the 1915 fight in Cuba against Willard, Johnson was knocked out in round 26, but this loss is asterisked: Johnson was said to have claimed he threw the fight. Many thought he did so in the hope of having the charges dropped and being allowed back onto American soil after dispatching a string of Great White Hopes. Maybe his early dominance in the bout was to make a point before he surrendered to the realities of his

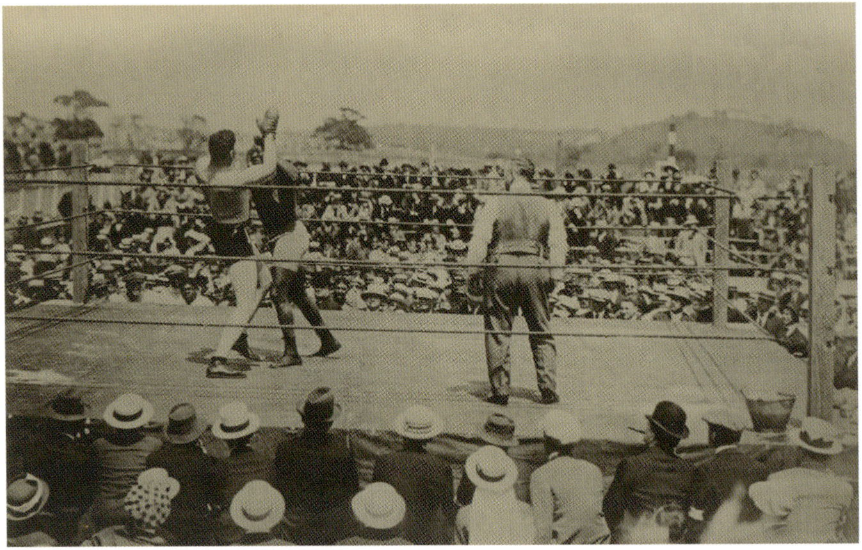

Jack Johnson vs. Jess Willard, Cuba, April 5, 1915
Unidentified photographer

nation. Maybe he lost. It is hard to land on an actual truth by looking at a single photograph.

Even though many of these pictures demand that you consider their larger social context, in several the joy of the game is still evident. The photo of a sandlot baseball game from the mid-1940s (see p. 28) epitomizes the new opportunities to compete during the Great Migration. The boy leaning against the fence in the back grabs my attention. He looks smooth, but ready should circumstances change. His confidence looks battle tested. His cool stance feels benevolent, like he's doing more for the clothes than they are for him. He gazes at the batter, whose lopsided, never-had-a-coach swing seems unpredictable. The boys are all way too well dressed for sandlot baseball. They are dressed for where they are going or where they came from, but this is where they want to be. In competition, camaraderie, and community they are like the fence slats behind them—jagged, unique, and stronger together.

Athletes, like photographers, are artists, and sports is an artform and medium of expression as central to the history and culture of Black people in America as music, poetry, and theater, and just as loaded with beautiful melodies, sharp allegories, and raw monologues. They are the kinds of things that young girls can sometimes capture in the whirring eye of a Double Dutch rope.

PHOTOGRAPHS

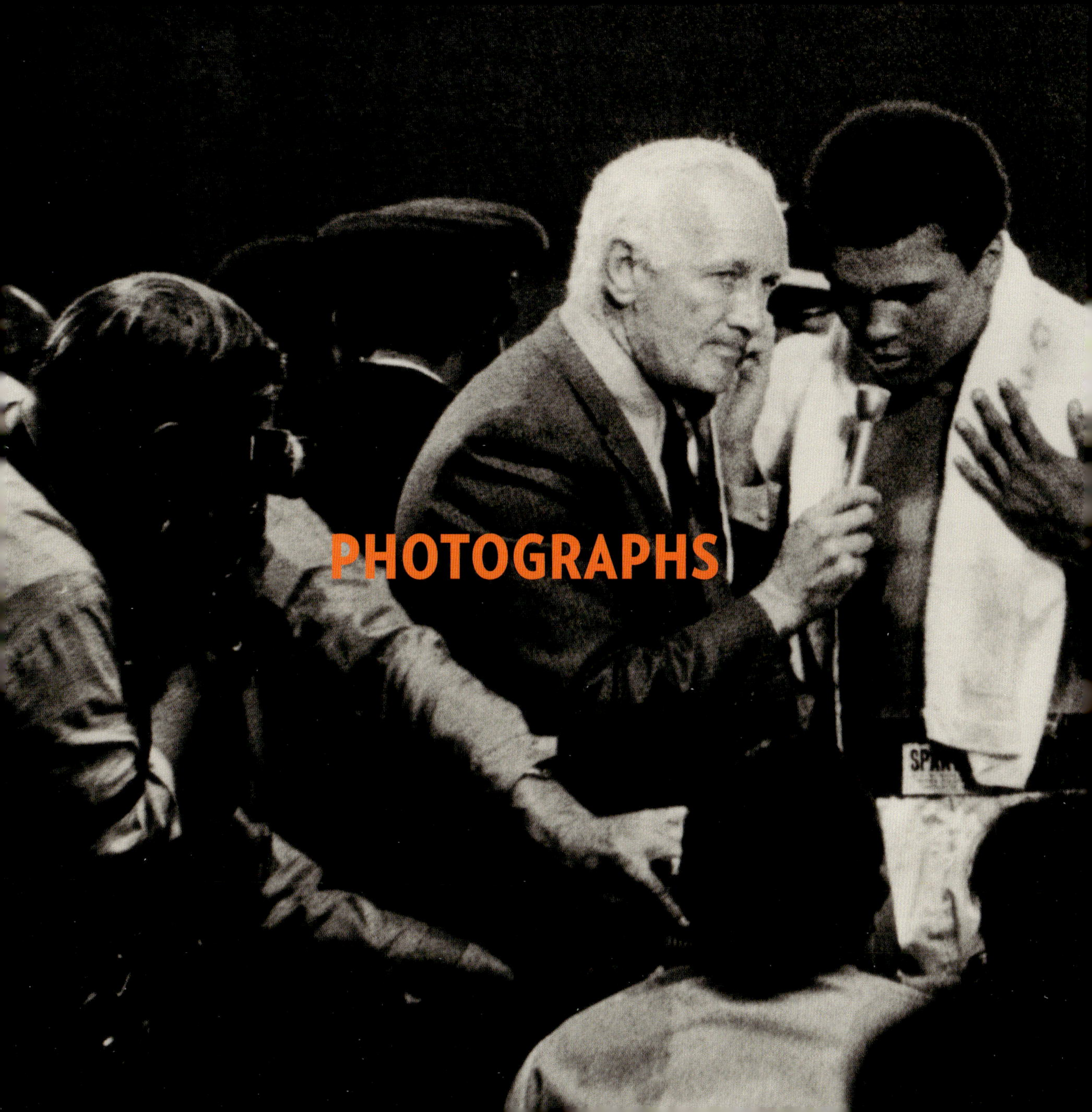

SURVIVAL AND COMMUNITY BUILDING: 1900–1945

Jack Johnson vs. Jim Jeffries, Reno, Nevada, July 4, 1910
Percy Dana Studio

—

In 1910, "The Fight of the Century" captivated America as it pitted Jack Johnson, the first African American World Heavyweight Champion, against Jim Jeffries, a previously undefeated World Heavyweight Champion. Johnson defeated the "Great White Hope" in the fifteenth round when Jeffries's corner threw in the towel. Johnson's victory sparked race riots across the nation, which resulted in more than ten African American deaths.

"The reason Jack Johnson was so beset by his own country . . . was because of his Unforgivable Blackness."

W. E. B. Du Bois

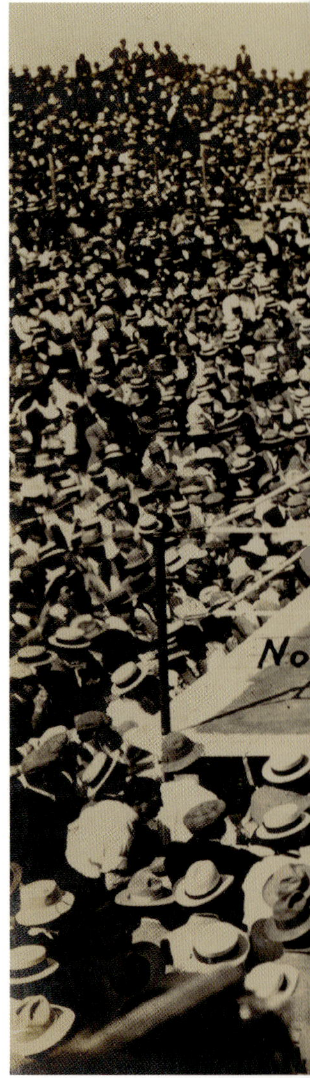

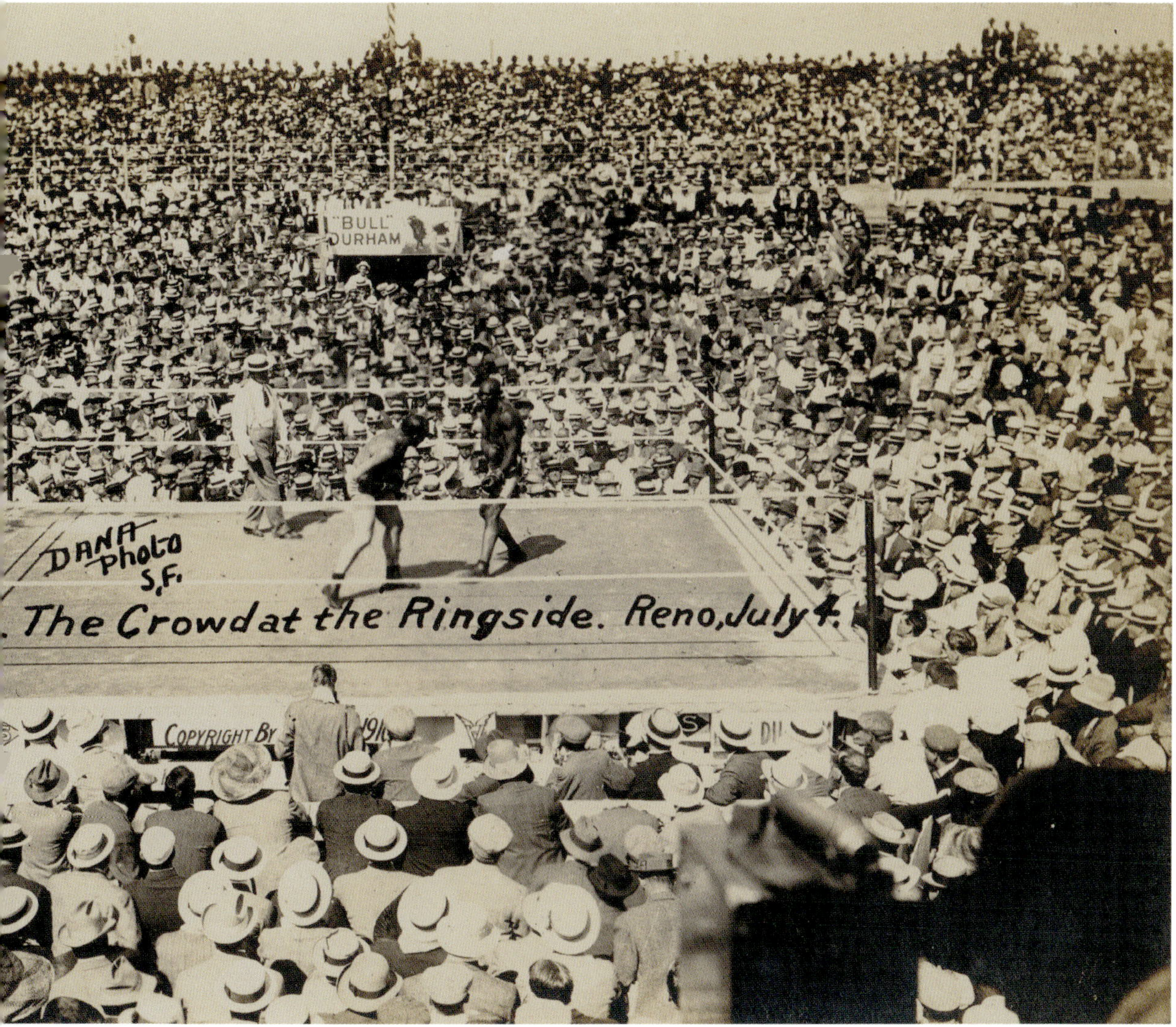
"BULL" DURHAM
DANA Photo S.F.
The Crowd at the Ringside. Reno, July 4.
COPYRIGHT BY

Aaron Molyneaux Hewlett, gymnasium coach at Harvard University, 1859–71
George Kendall Warren

—

Aaron Molyneaux Hewlett, a porter and boxing coach, served as a physical education instructor and the first African American director of the Harvard College gymnasium. He represents African American interest in an emerging field in the early twentieth century: physical education.

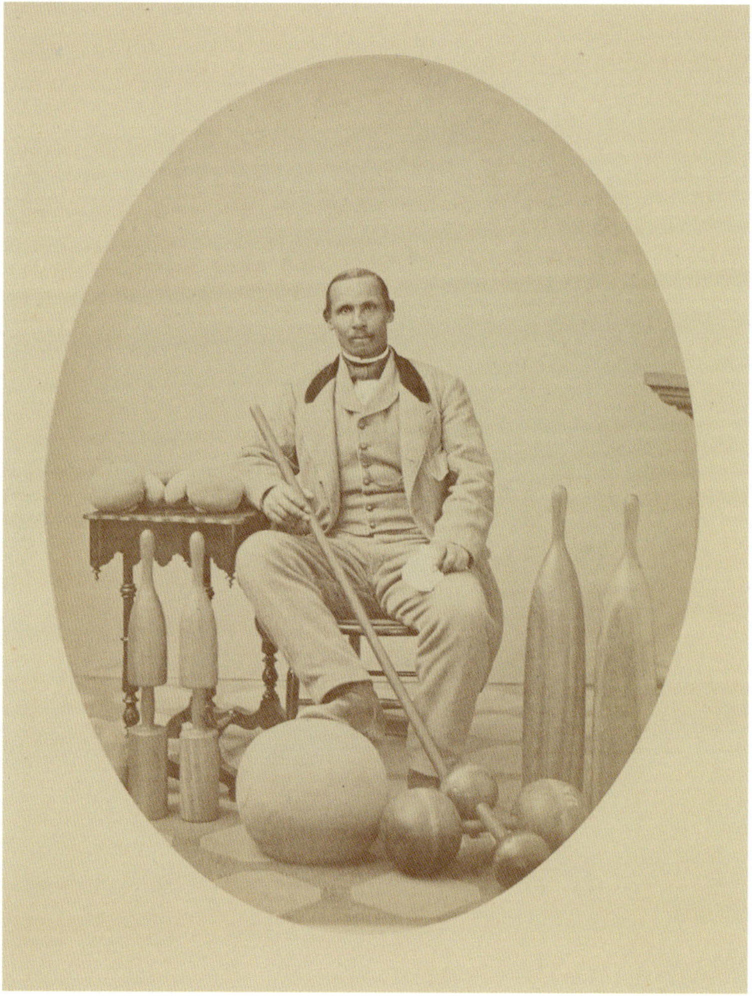

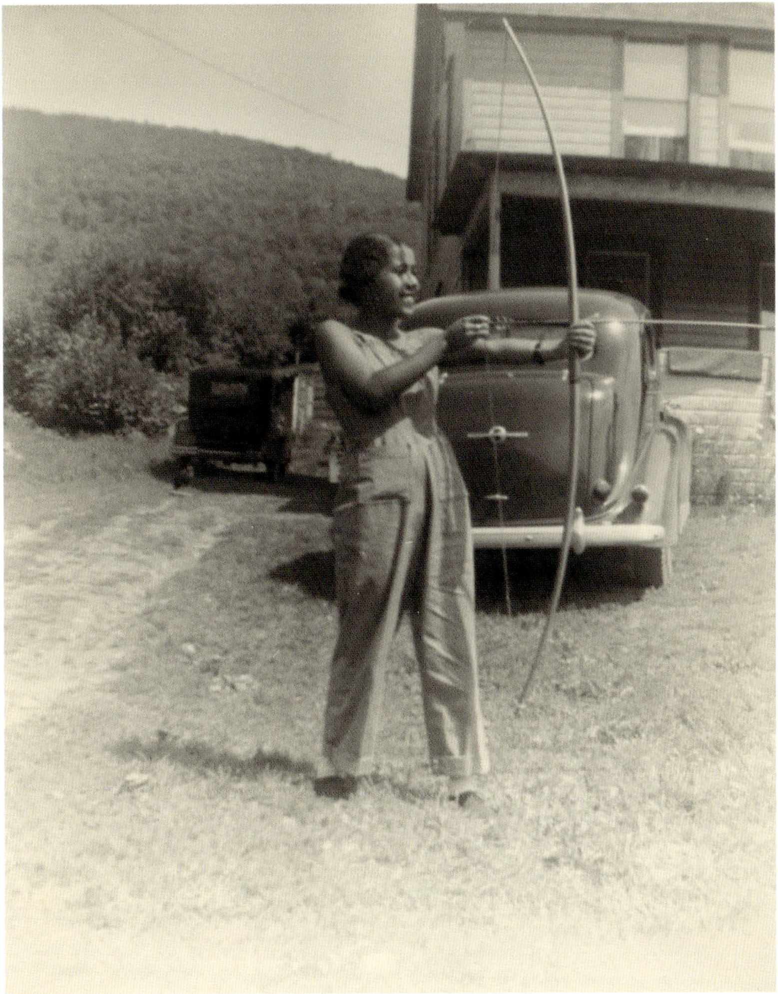

A young woman with a bow and arrow,
1940s
Unidentified photographer

—

This young woman's interest in archery exemplifies the varied sports that African Americans engaged in during the early to mid-twentieth century. African Americans carved out a vibrant, diverse sporting culture that was essential to their mental wellbeing, physical health, and sense of community.

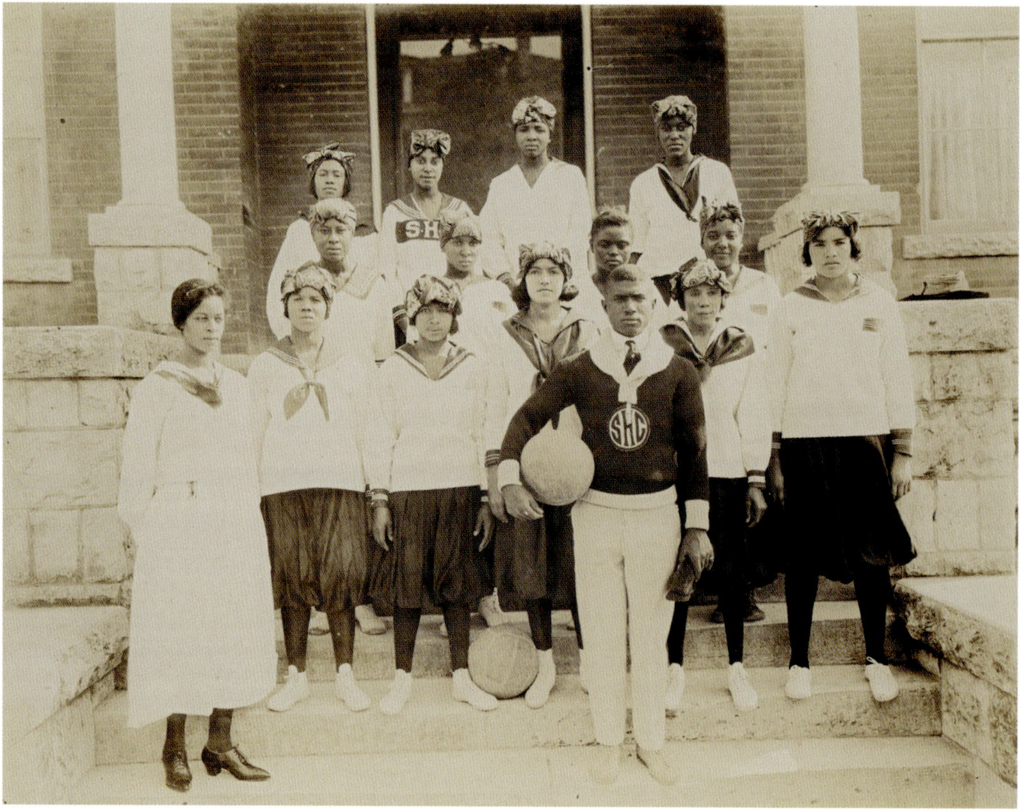

Samuel Huston College women's basketball team, 1920s
Unidentified photographer

—

Samuel Huston College and other Historically Black Colleges and Universities were much more likely to include women's athletics than predominantly white colleges and universities during the first half of the twentieth century.

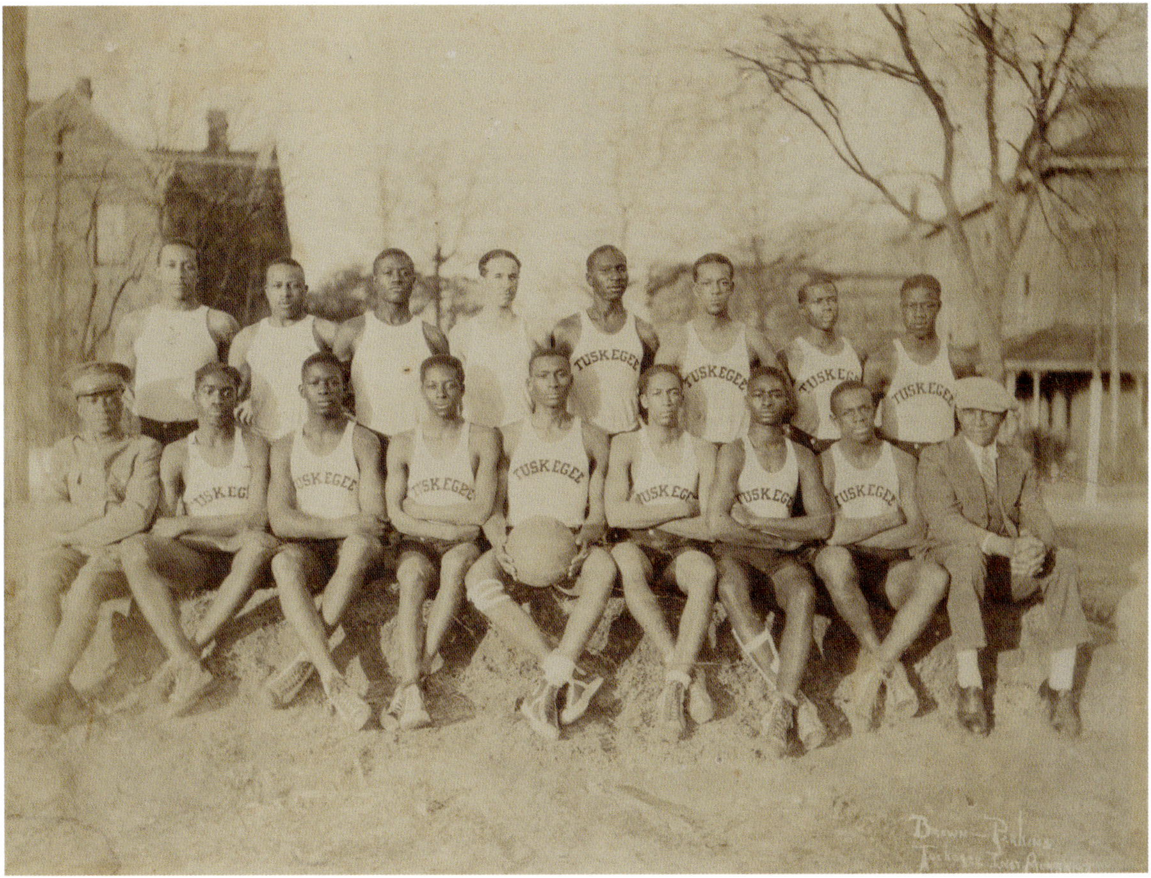

Tuskegee Institute men's basketball team, 1929
Brown-Perkins

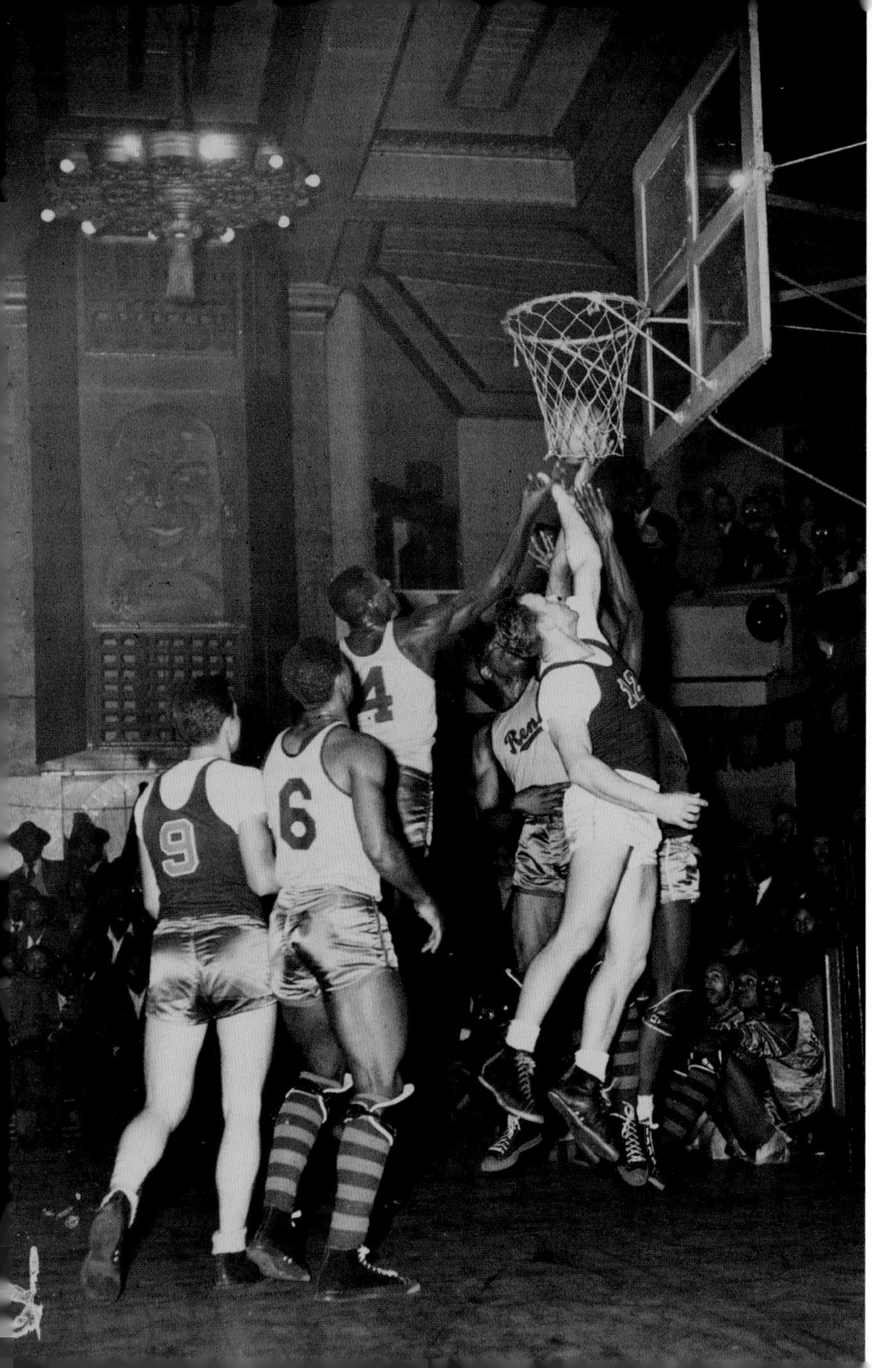

New York Rens basketball game at the Renaissance Casino, November 6, 1946
Unidentified photographer

—

The New York Rens were named for the Renaissance Casino and Ballroom in Harlem, New York, in exchange for use of the hall for their home games. They played basketball games before dances and other events in the ballroom.

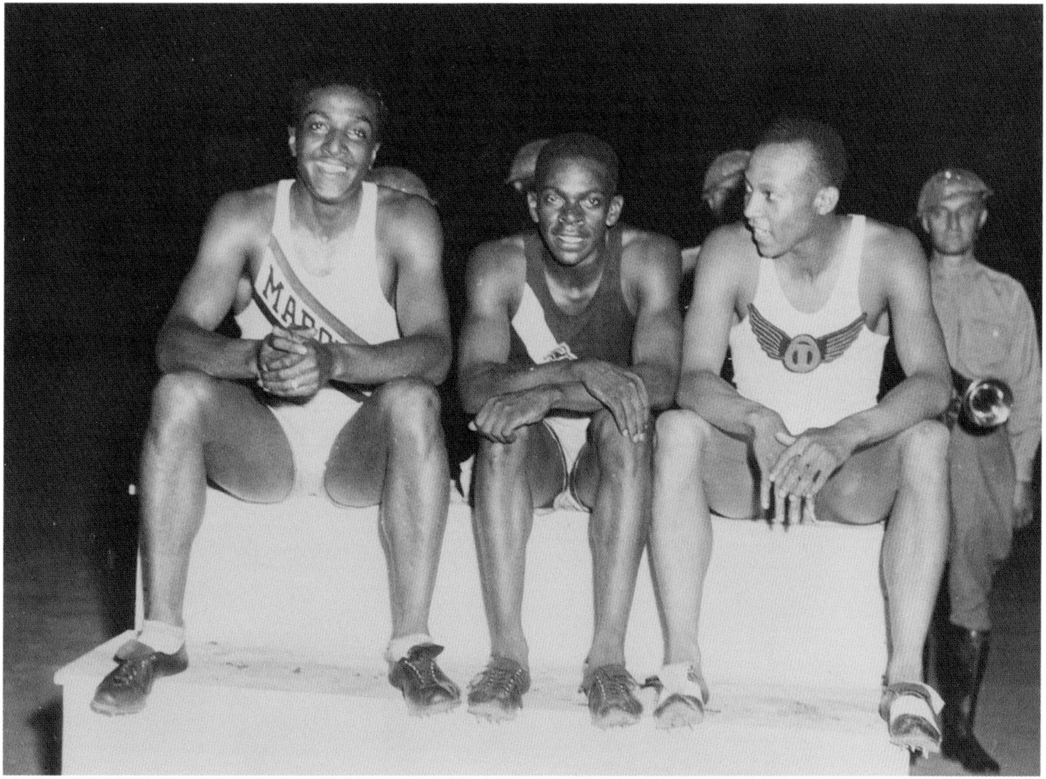

Ralph Metcalfe, James Johnson, and Jesse Owens before the 100-meter race at the Amateur Athletic Union Track and Field Championships in Chicago, Illinois, July 30, 1933
Acme
—

Ralph Metcalfe (left) defeated Jesse Owens (right) at the 1933 AAU Championship. However, at the 1936 Olympic Games in Berlin, Owens won gold and Metcalfe won silver in the 100-meter dash.

A young boxer at Eddie Nichols Gymnasium, 1946–48
From the series **The Way of Life of the Northern Negro**
Wayne F. Miller

—

Eddie Nichols Gymnasium was a popular gym for young boxers on the South Side of Chicago, Illinois. Many of the young men who trained there were recent transplants whose families traveled north during the Great Migration.

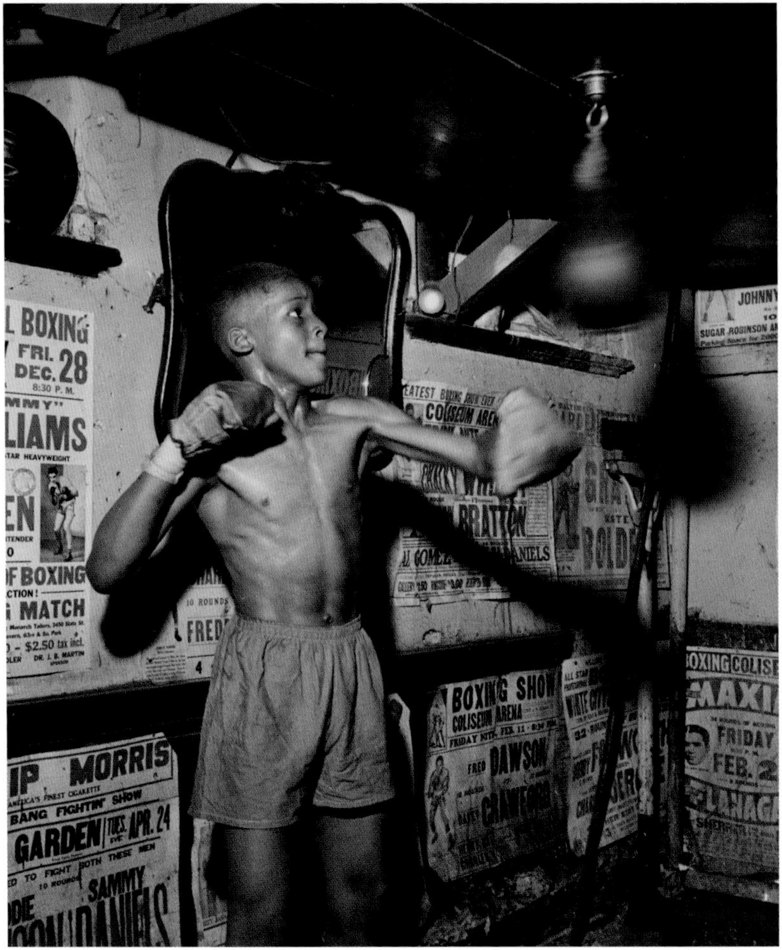

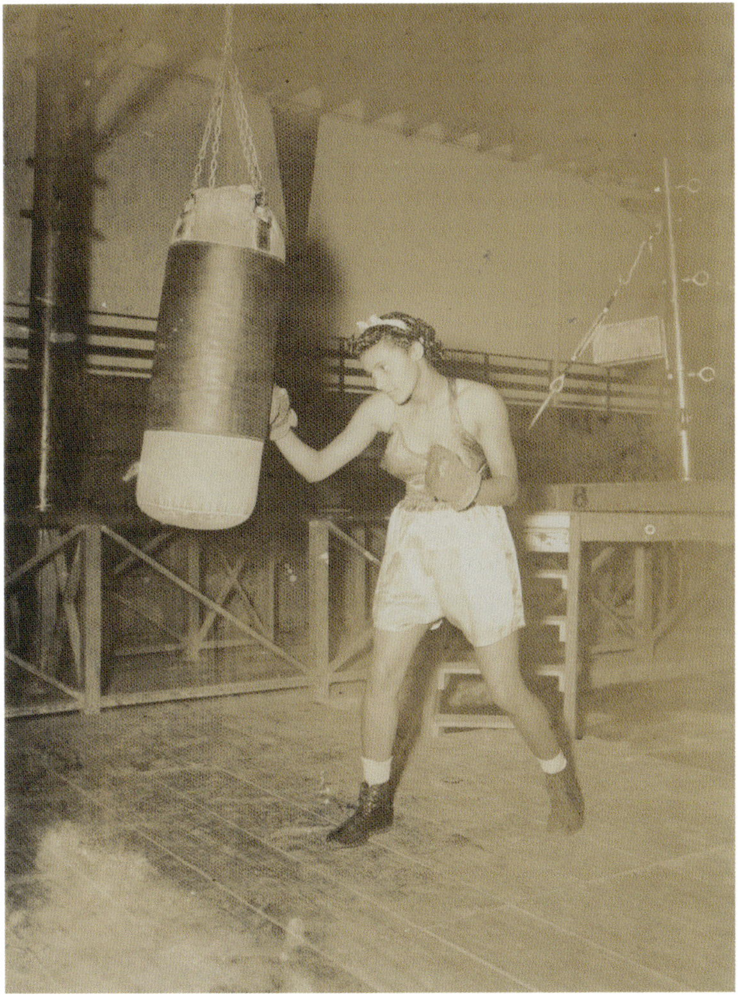

Emma Maitland, late 1920s; printed later
Unidentified photographer

—

Emma Maitland was a dance teacher who moved to Paris and danced at the Moulin Rouge after her husband, Clarence Maitland, died during their first year of marriage. According to family lore, she started boxing to rebuff unwanted advances while dancing at events. She earned over $500 per fight and became the female lightweight boxing champion of the world.

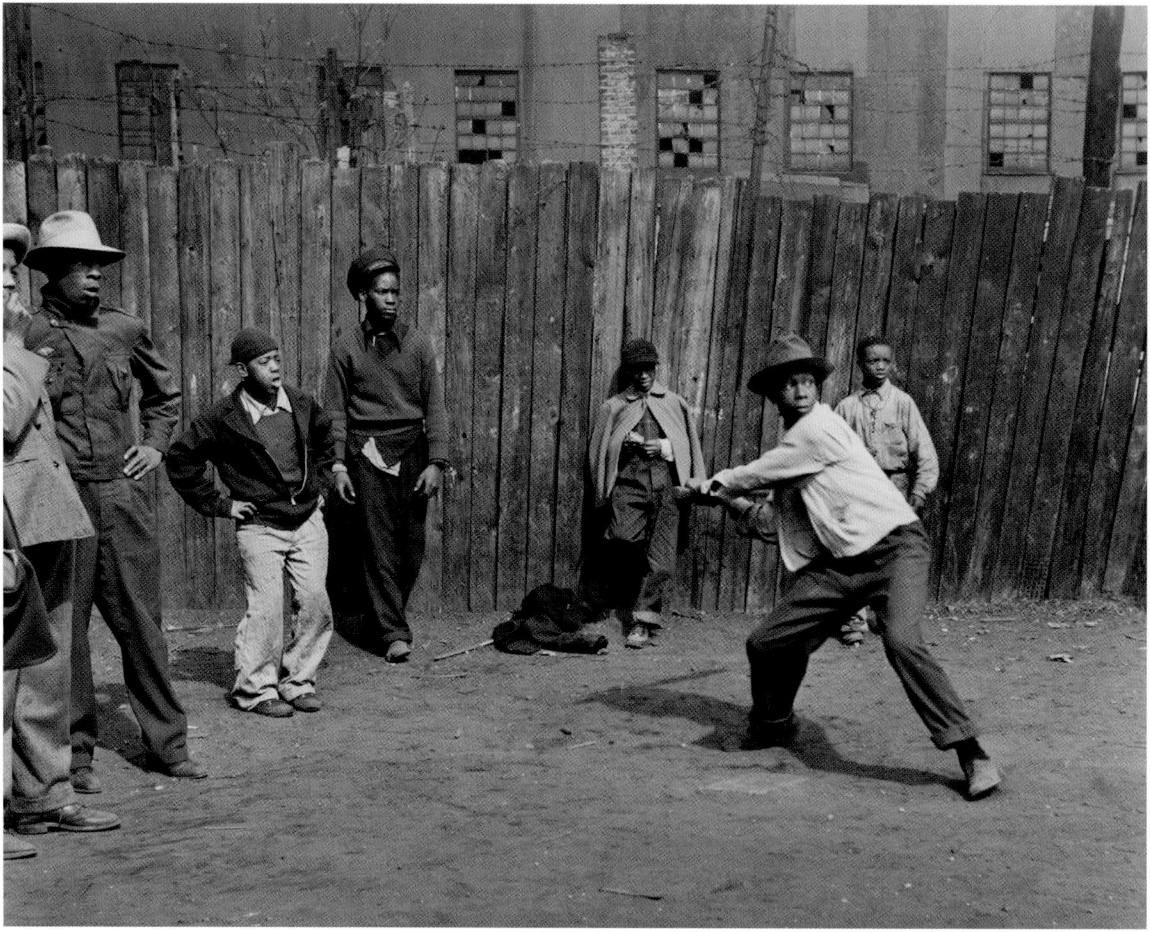

Sandlot baseball, Chicago, 1946–48
From the series **The Way of Life of the Northern Negro**
Wayne F. Miller

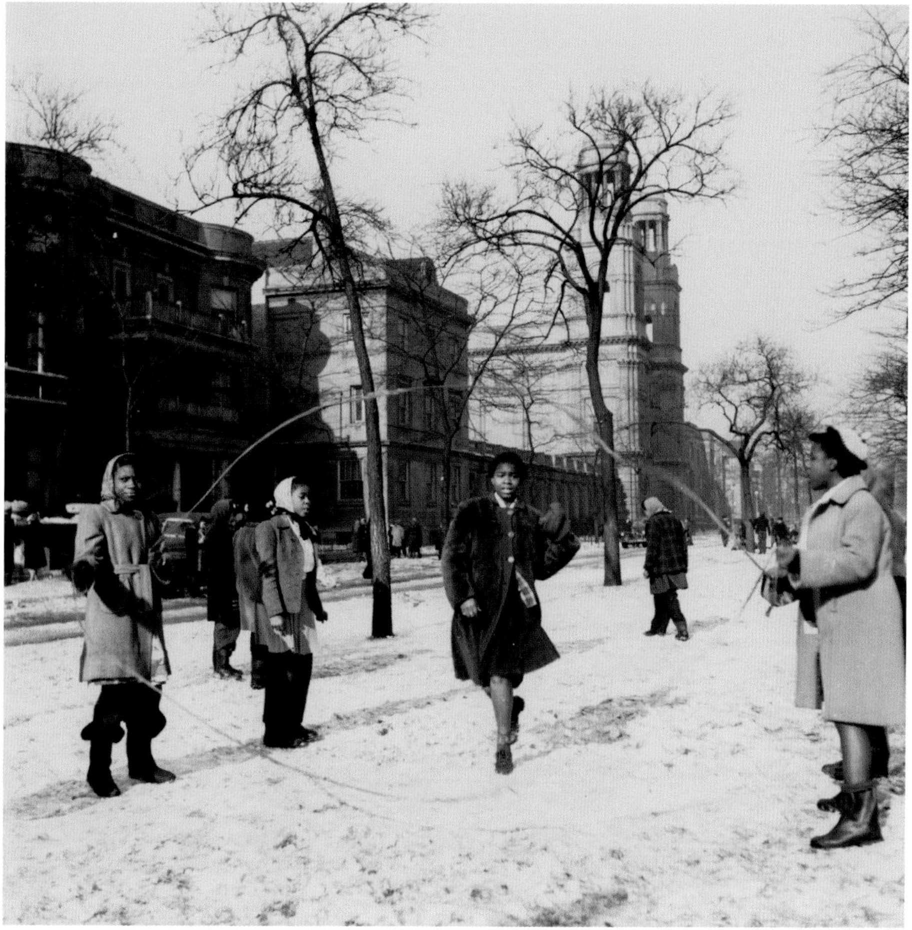

Double Dutch, Chicago, 1946–48; printed later
From the series **The Way of Life of the Northern Negro**
Wayne F. Miller
—

Double Dutch became a favored sport, especially for girls, during the Depression era because it was inexpensive: it only required a clothesline, unlike most of the games and sports children in middle-class families played.

STRUGGLE AND BREAKTHROUGH: 1945–1968

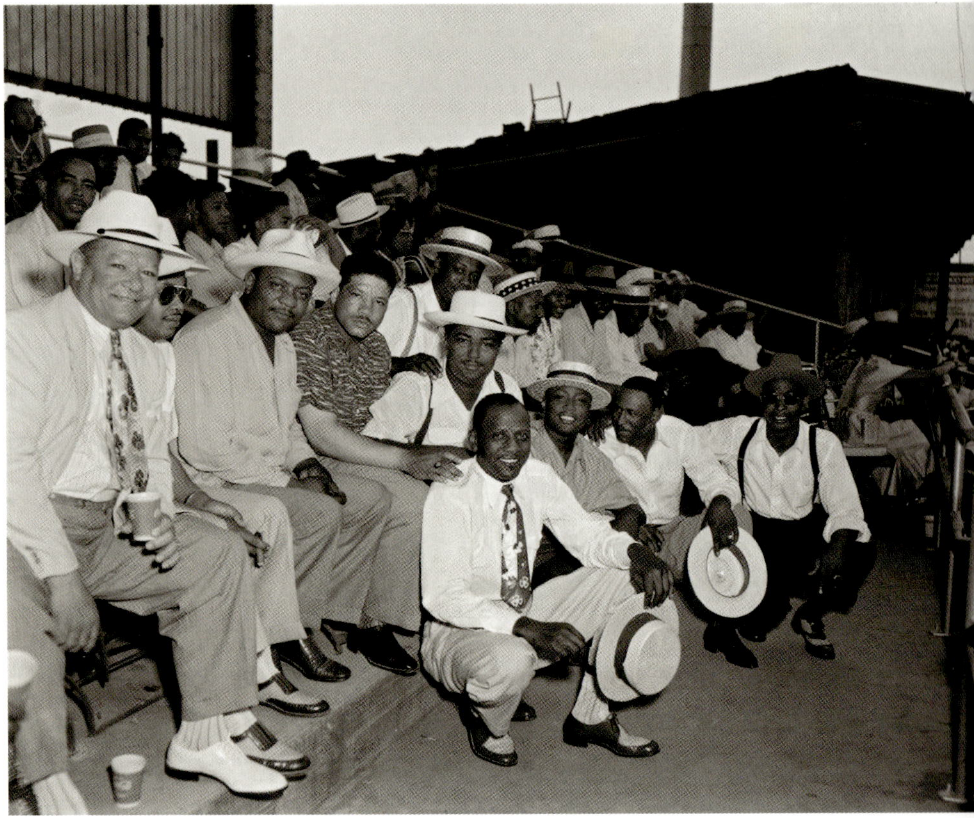

Larry Brown with Fans, Martin Stadium, Memphis, TN, ca. 1945
Ernest C. Withers

—

Larry Brown (center, without hat), a famed catcher in the Negro Leagues, poses at Martin Stadium, then the only stadium owned by African Americans in the United States. Brothers John B. Martin, B.B. Martin, and William S. Martin owned the stadium and the Memphis Red Sox. Even though Martin Stadium was Black owned, it hosted political, religious, and community events for white and Black patrons.

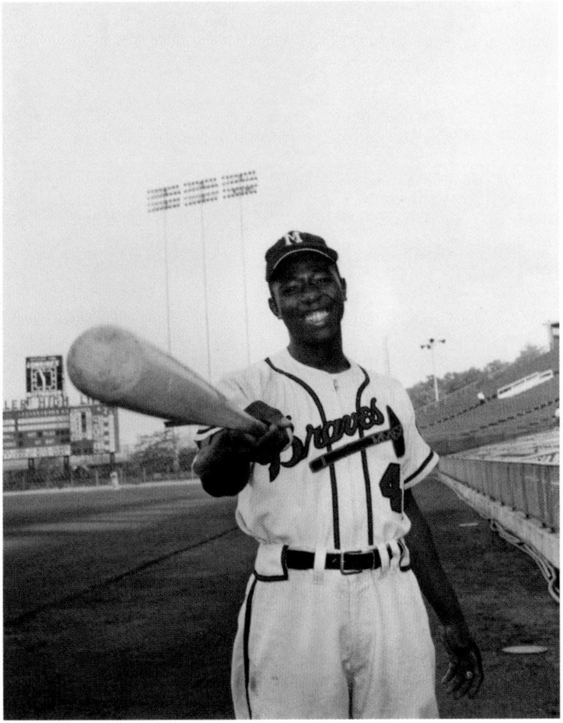

Hank Aaron, ca. 1956
David Jackson

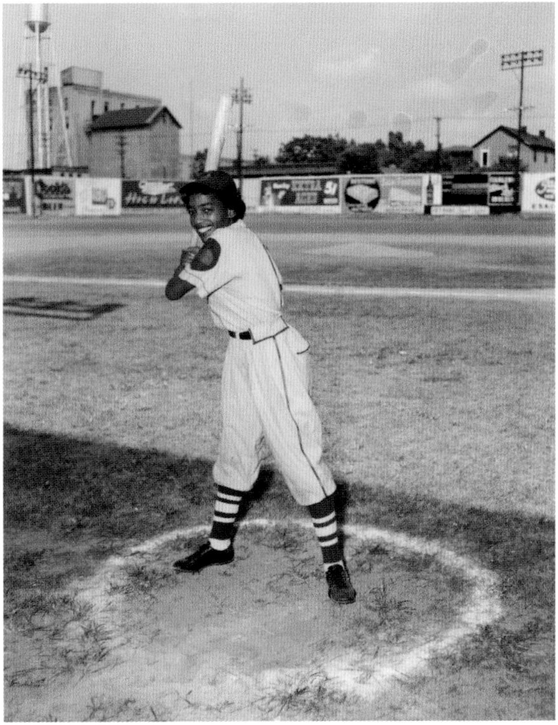

Connie Morgan, Martin Stadium, Memphis, TN, ca. 1954
Ernest C. Withers

Willie Mays at Camp Kilmer, New Jersey, May 31, 1952
U.S. Army

—

Like many other Major League Baseball players, Willie Mays was called into military service during the Korean War. His service obligation caused him to miss 266 games during the early part of his career.

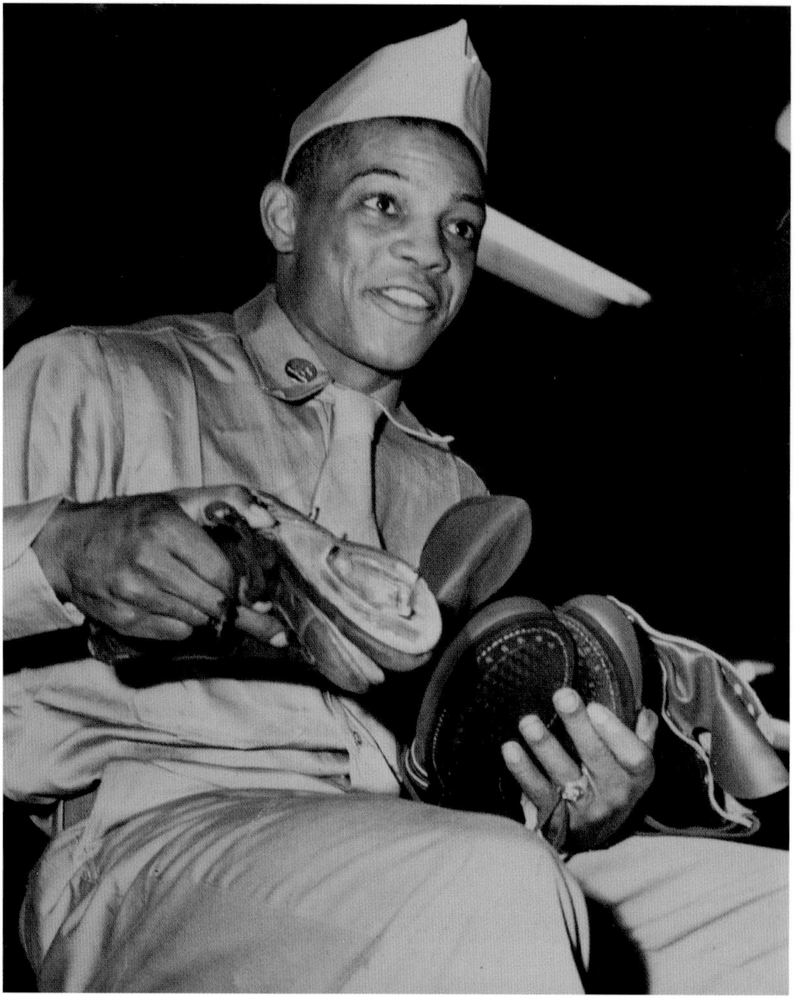

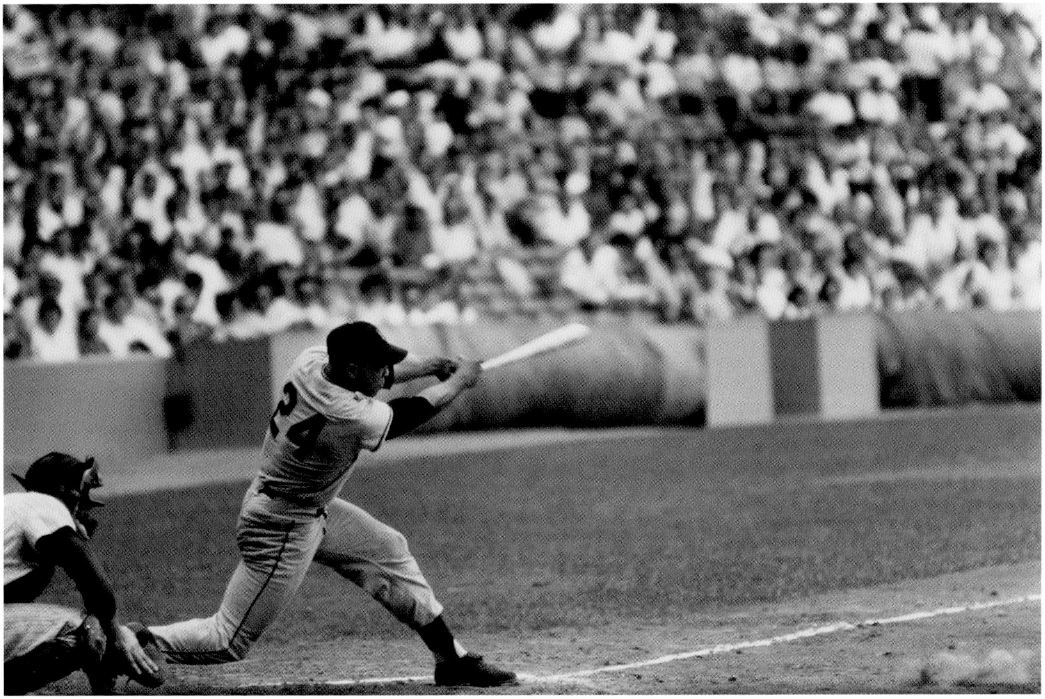

Willie Mays, Philadelphia, 1962
Walter Iooss Jr.
—

Willie Mays, among the first wave of African American players to follow Jackie Robinson into Major League Baseball, fashioned a Hall of Fame career with the New York/San Francisco Giants that included 3,005 games, 660 home runs, and 3,283 hits over 22 seasons.

Jackie Robinson stealing home, May 18, 1952
International News Photo

—

Jackie Robinson did not allow the fact that he was the first African American to play modern Major League Baseball, or that he was on the receiving end of some of the worst forms of racial epithets, to impact the way he played the game. He competed on the diamond with almost total abandon, diving for ground balls and running the bases with unparalleled aggression, and stealing home nineteen times in regular seasons and once in the World Series. These three photographs show Robinson stealing home in the Brooklyn Dodgers' May 18, 1952, game against the Chicago Cubs. The photo editor at the New Amsterdam News, a Black-owned newspaper in New York City, attached these photographs together so they could be cropped and reproduced as a banner across the top of a page in the newspaper's May 24 issue.

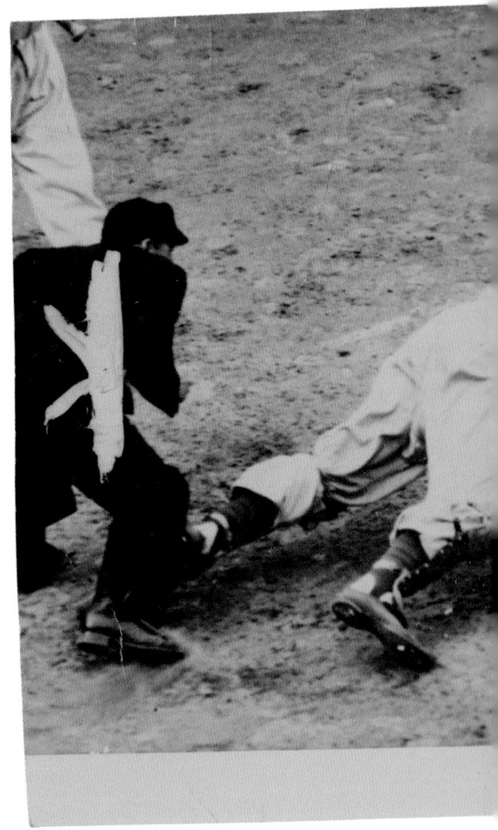

"I don't think that I or any other Negro, as an American citizen, should have to ask for anything that is rightfully his. We are demanding that we just be given the things that are rightfully ours and that we're not looking for anything else."

Jackie Robinson

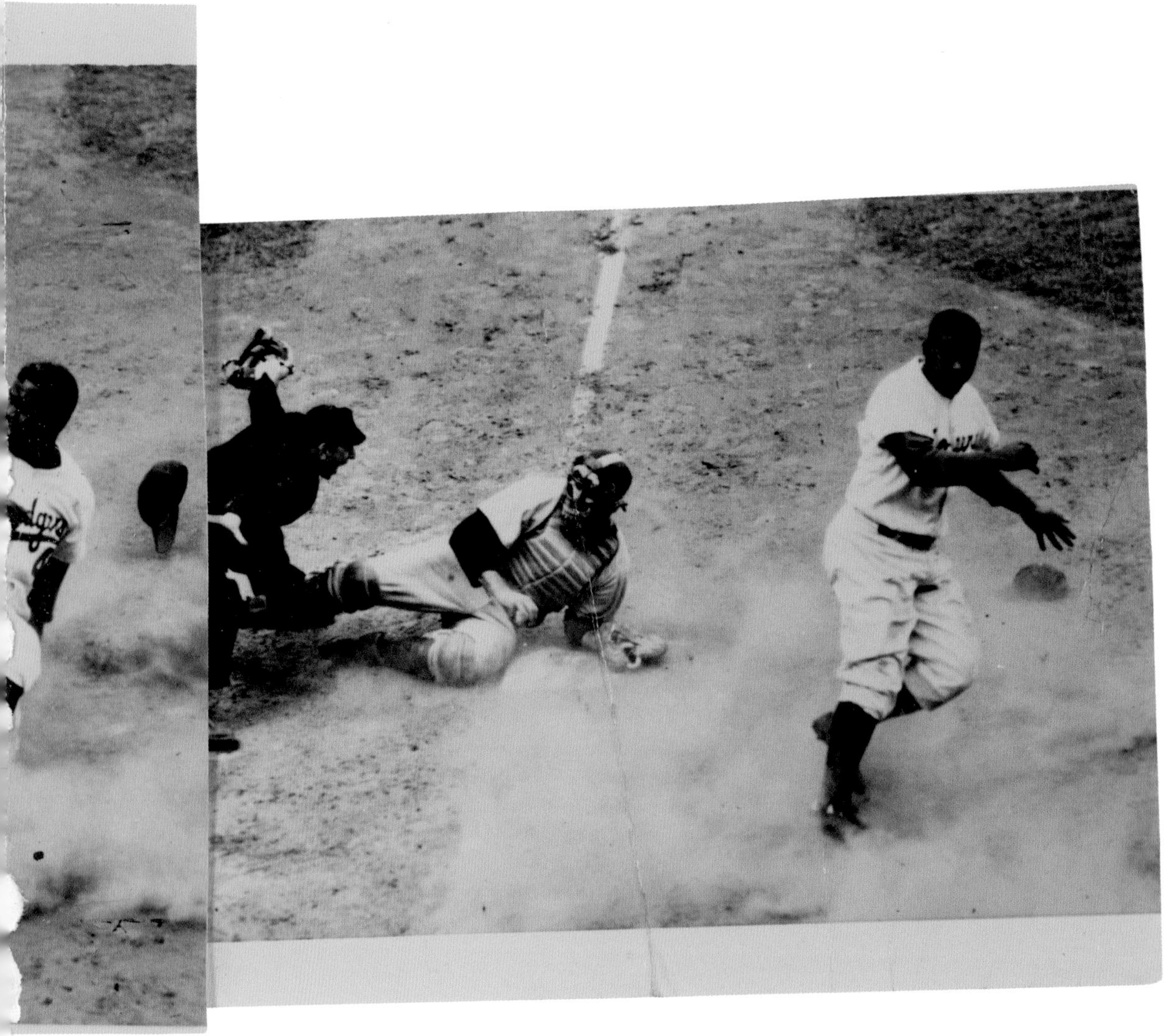

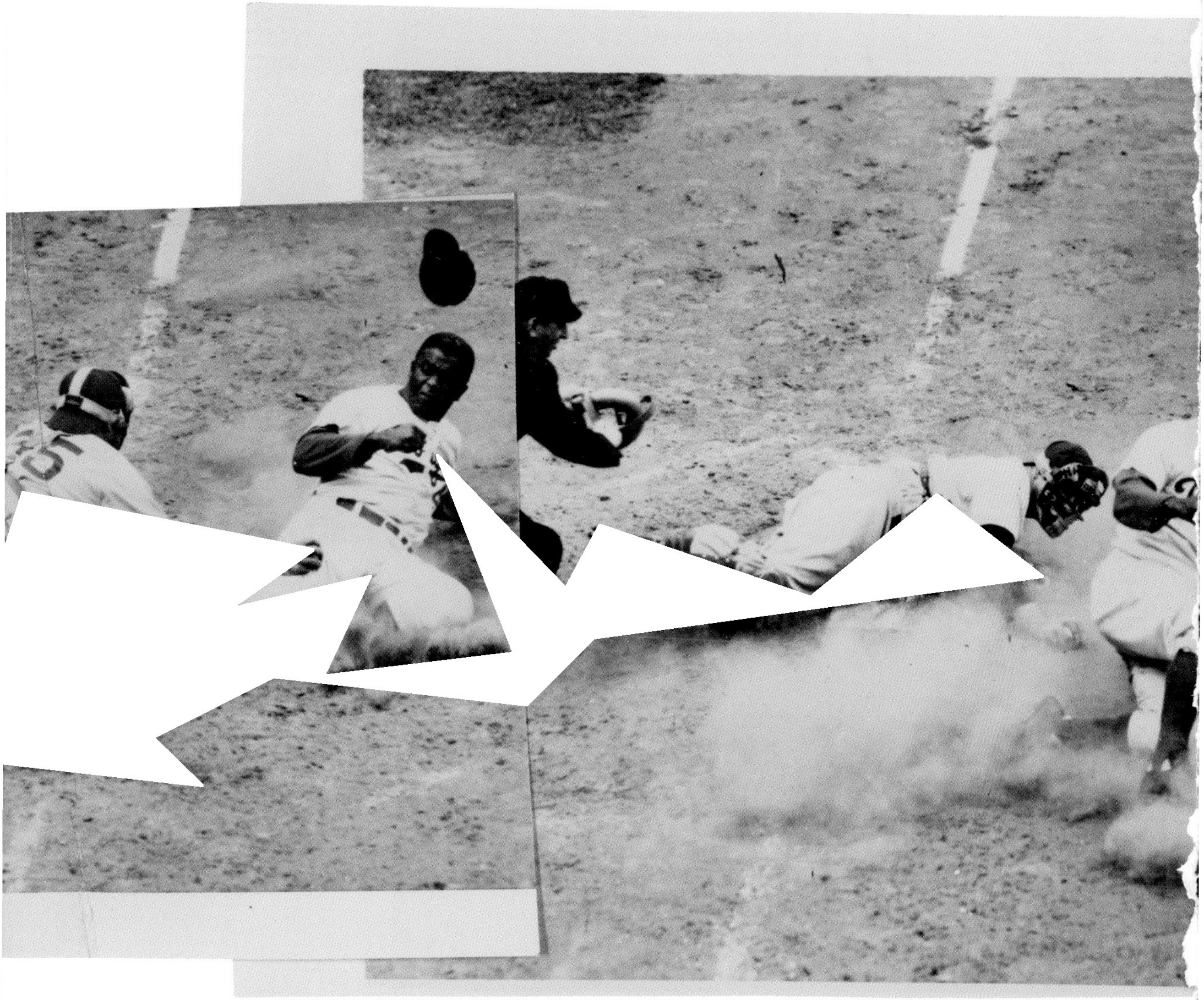

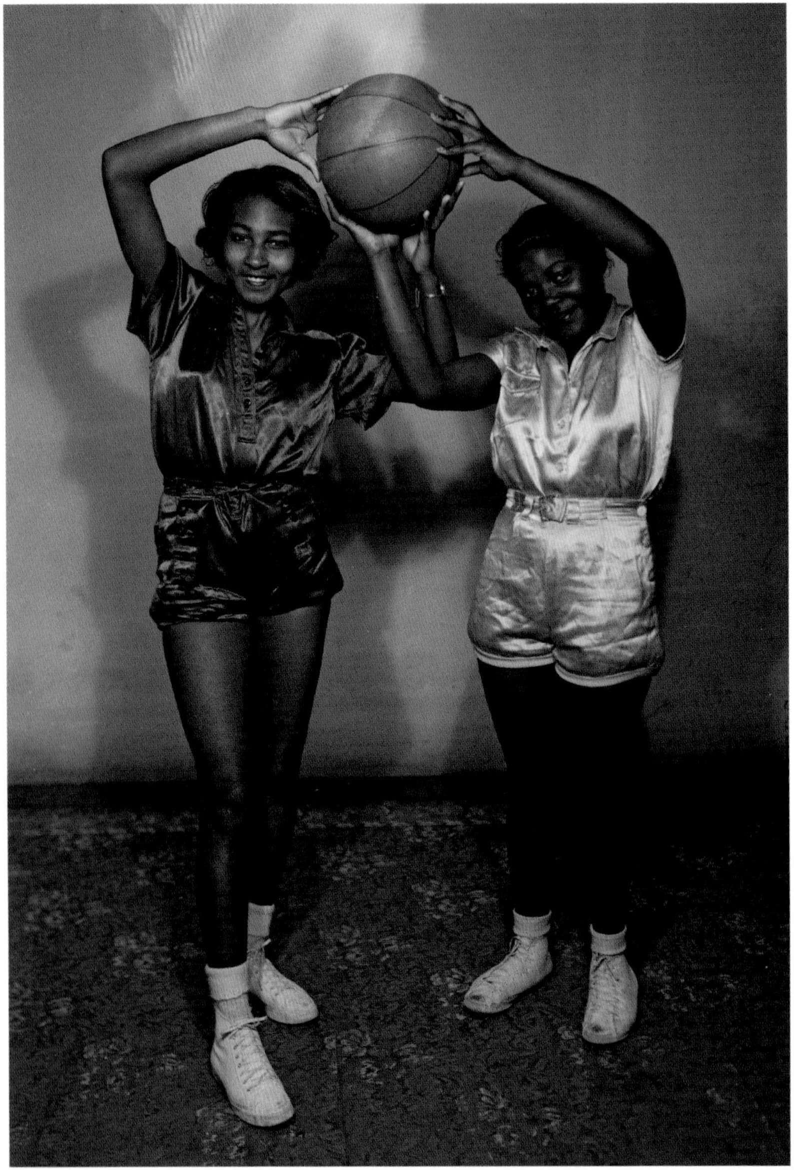

Two girls holding a basketball, mid-20th century
Rev. Henry Clay Anderson

—

This photograph by Rev. Henry Clay Anderson is one of the many he took documenting the African American community in and around Greenville, Mississippi. Having their portrait taken in Anderson's studio demonstrates the athletes' pride in the game.

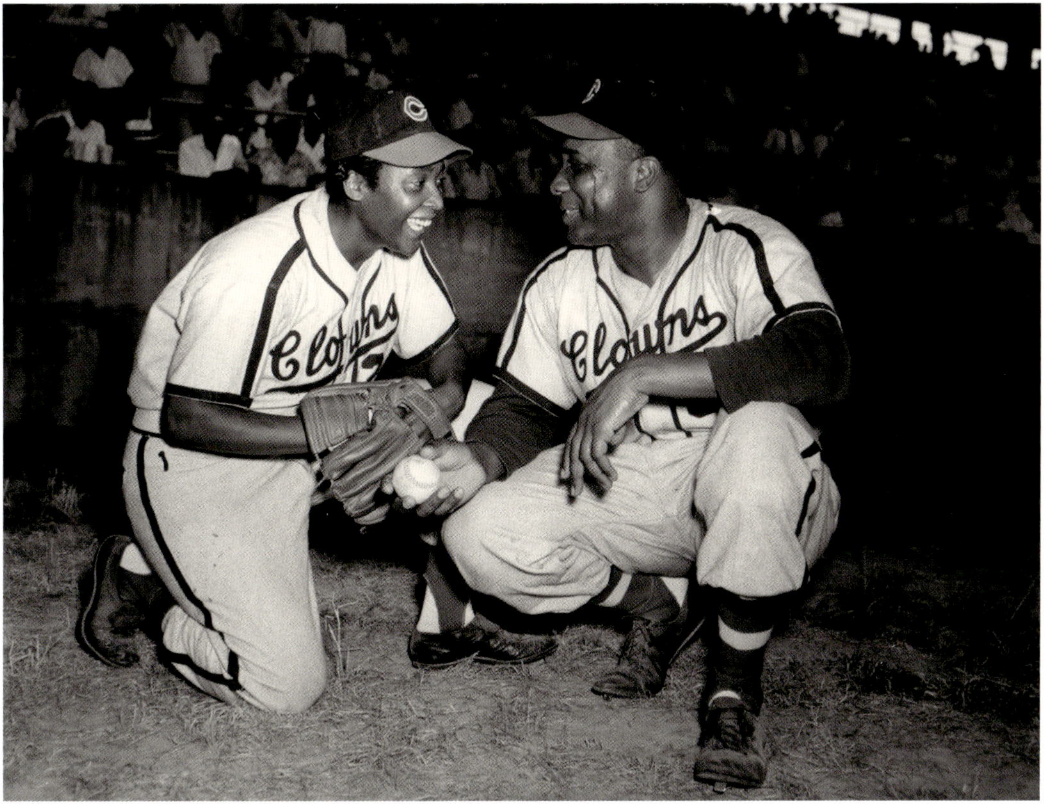

Marcia "Toni" Stone and Unidentified Teammate, Martin Stadium, Memphis, TN,
ca. 1954
Ernest C. Withers
—

Toni Stone (left) played for the Indianapolis Clowns of the Negro American League during the 1953 and 1954 seasons. She was the first of three women to play in the Negro Leagues, along with Mamie "Peanut" Johnson and Connie Morgan.

Gloria King at the Cosmopolitan Tennis Club, ca. 1945
Unidentified photographer
—
The Cosmopolitan Tennis Club in Harlem was perhaps the most prestigious athletic and social club for African Americans in the early twentieth century. It served as an important center of social life for the African American elite and held tournaments sponsored by the American Tennis Association, a Black organization founded in 1916.

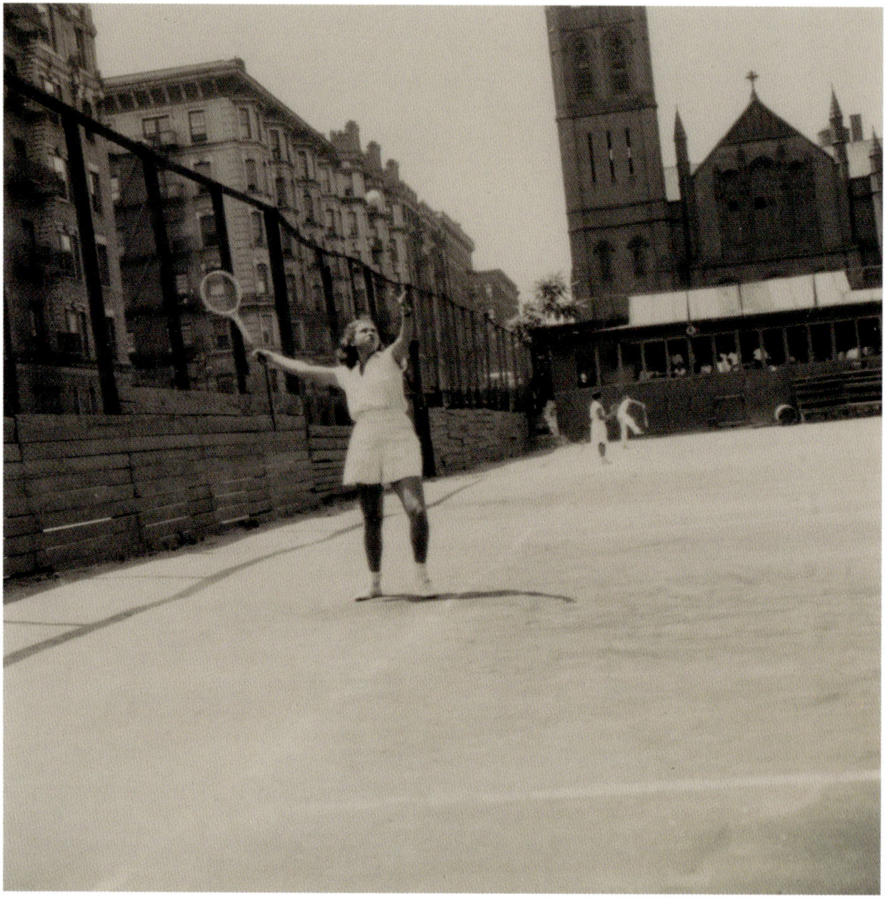

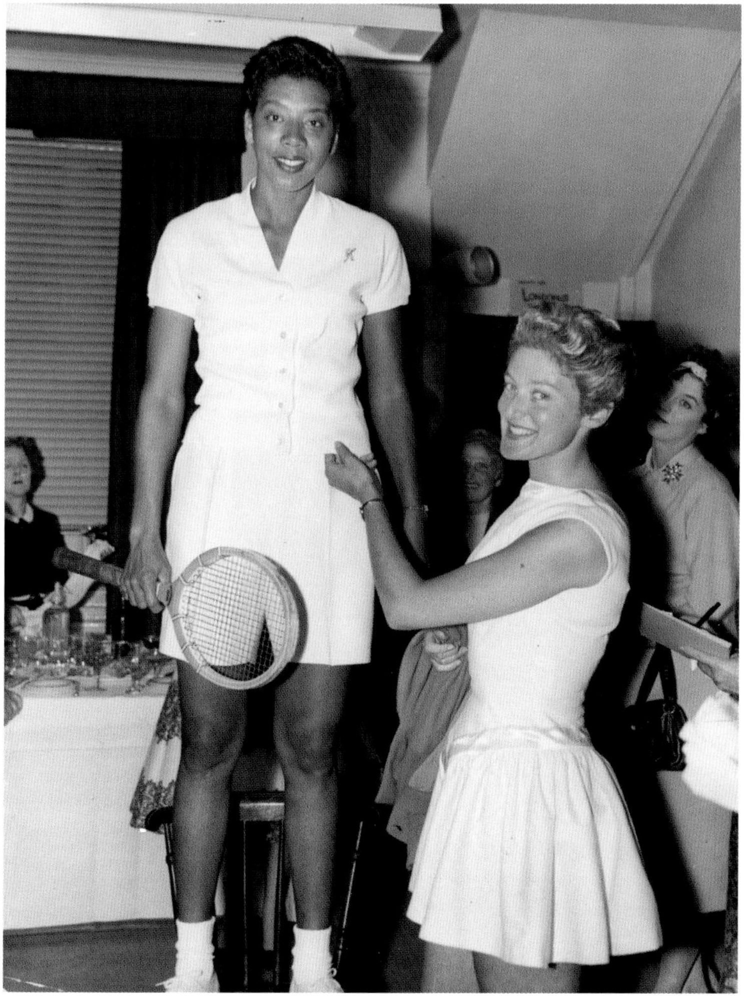

Althea Gibson and Angela Buxton, 1958
Unidentified photographer
—
Althea Gibson teamed up with England's Angela Buxton to capture the doubles titles at both the 1956 French Open and Wimbledon Championships. An injury Buxton suffered prevented them from competing together again for major titles.

A bowling team,
mid-20th century
Jimmy Baynes

—

Bowling was a popular sport among African American women during the mid-twentieth century. This photograph was taken by Jimmy Baynes, a Black postal worker known for photographing the African American community and music scene in Cleveland, Ohio, during the 1950s and 60s.

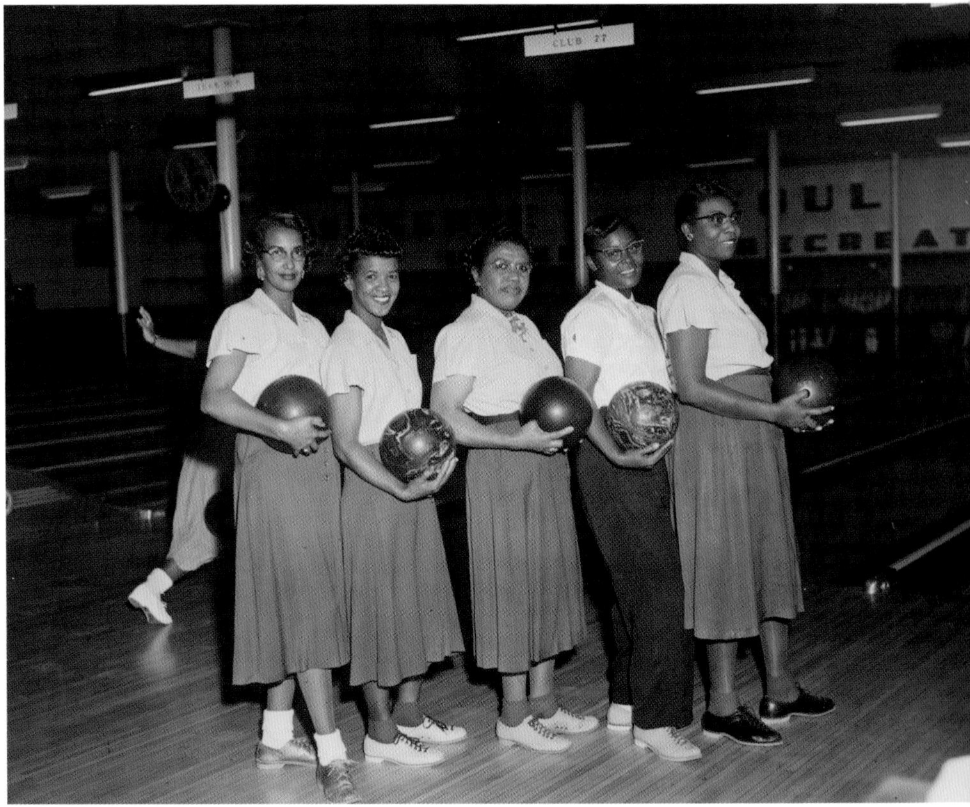

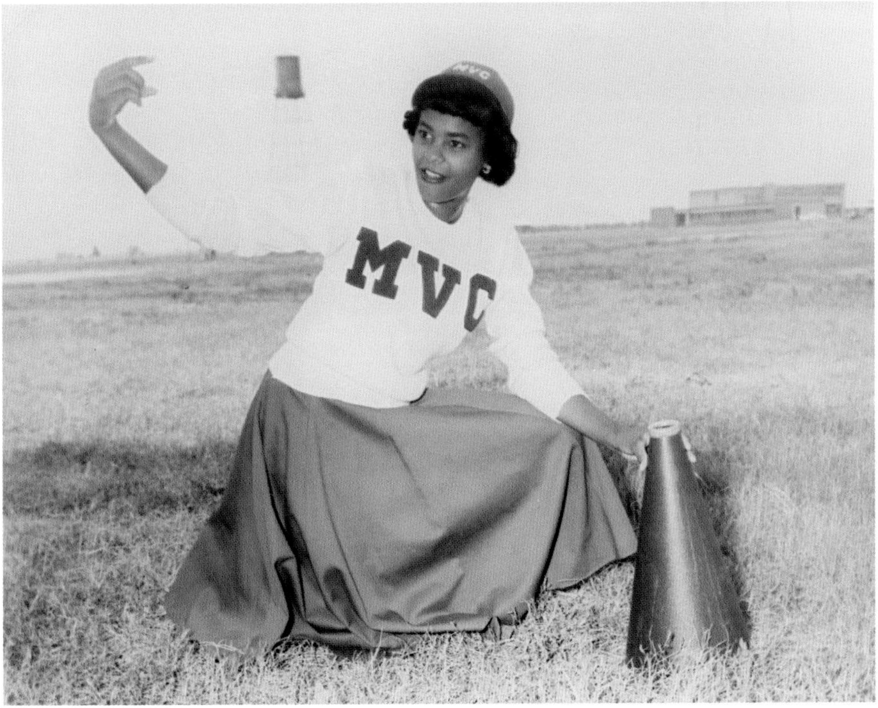

A Mississippi Vocational College cheerleader, 1950s
Rev. Henry Clay Anderson

—

Cheerleaders were integral aspects of the athletic programs at Historically Black Colleges and Universities, such as Mississippi Vocational College (now Mississippi Valley State University).

Wilt Chamberlain in class at the University of Kansas, 1957
David Jackson

—

Basketball great Wilt Chamberlain embraced student life at the University of Kansas, despite being one of the few African Americans on campus. Besides his work in the classroom, he joined the historically African American Kappa Alpha Psi Fraternity, Inc., and had his own thirty-minute weekly radio show "Flip'er with Dipper" where he played current hit music and bantered with invited guests.

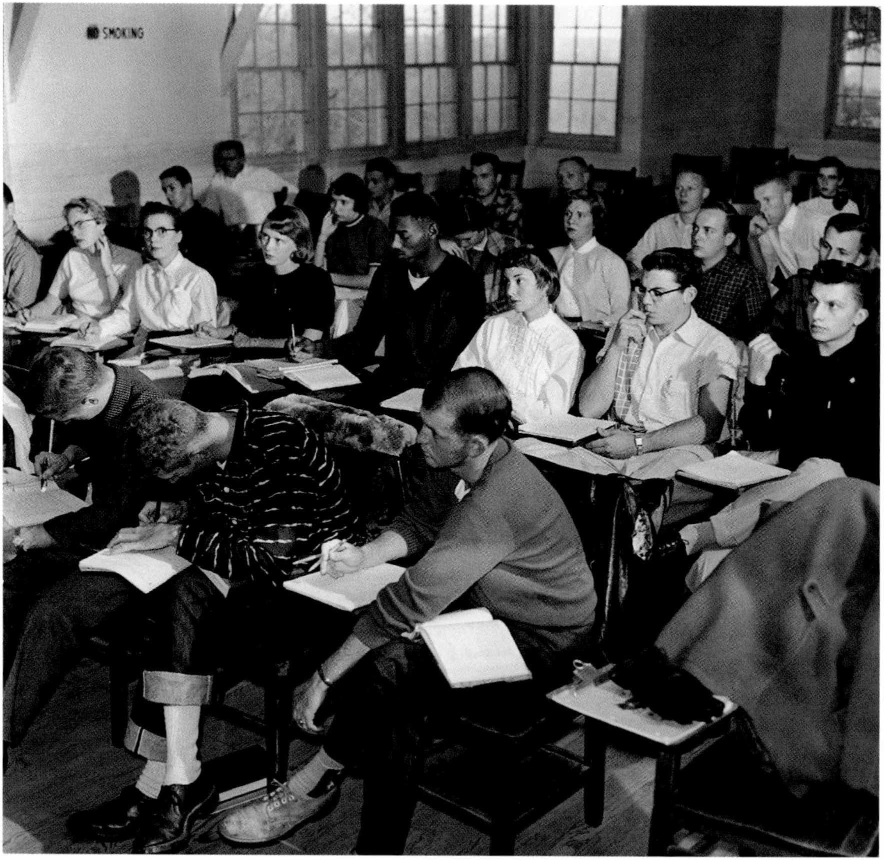

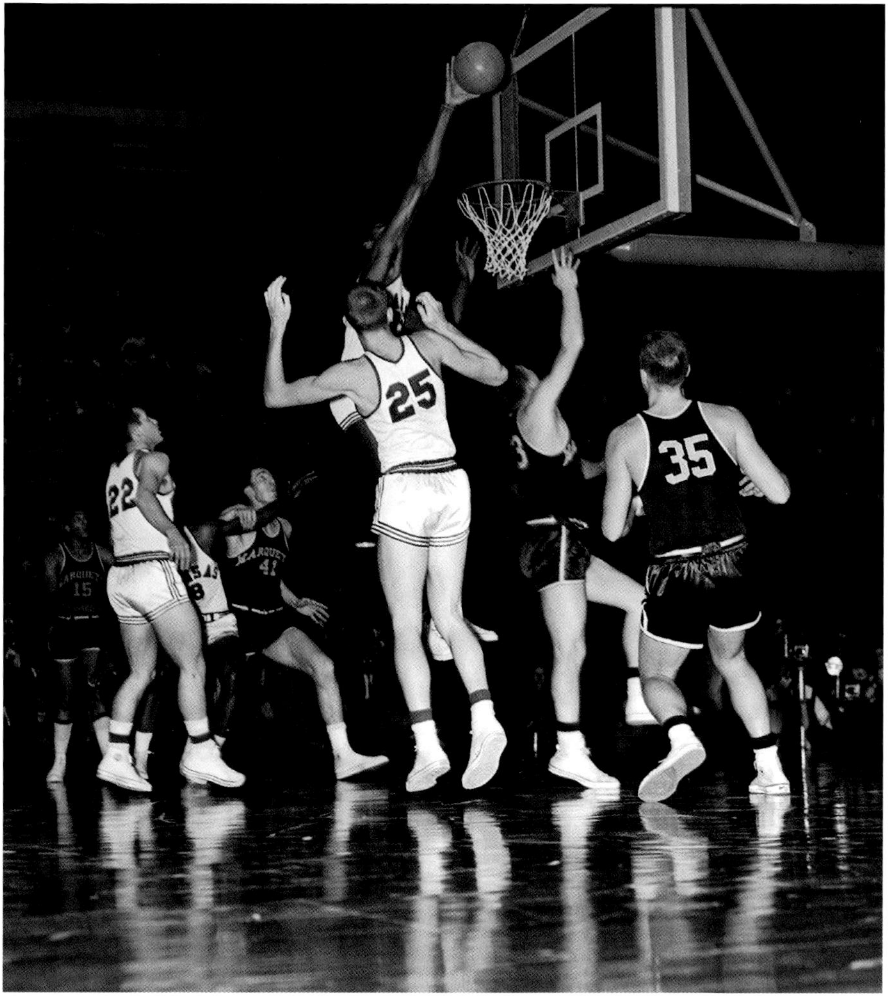

Wilt Chamberlain elevates during a University of Kansas basketball game against Marquette University, 1957
David Jackson

—

Wilt Chamberlain, with enormous strength and athleticism, was a force at the center position through high school, college, and his lengthy professional career. His on-court dominance was historic, including the incredible feat of scoring 100 points in a single game with the Philadelphia Warriors against the New York Knicks in 1962.

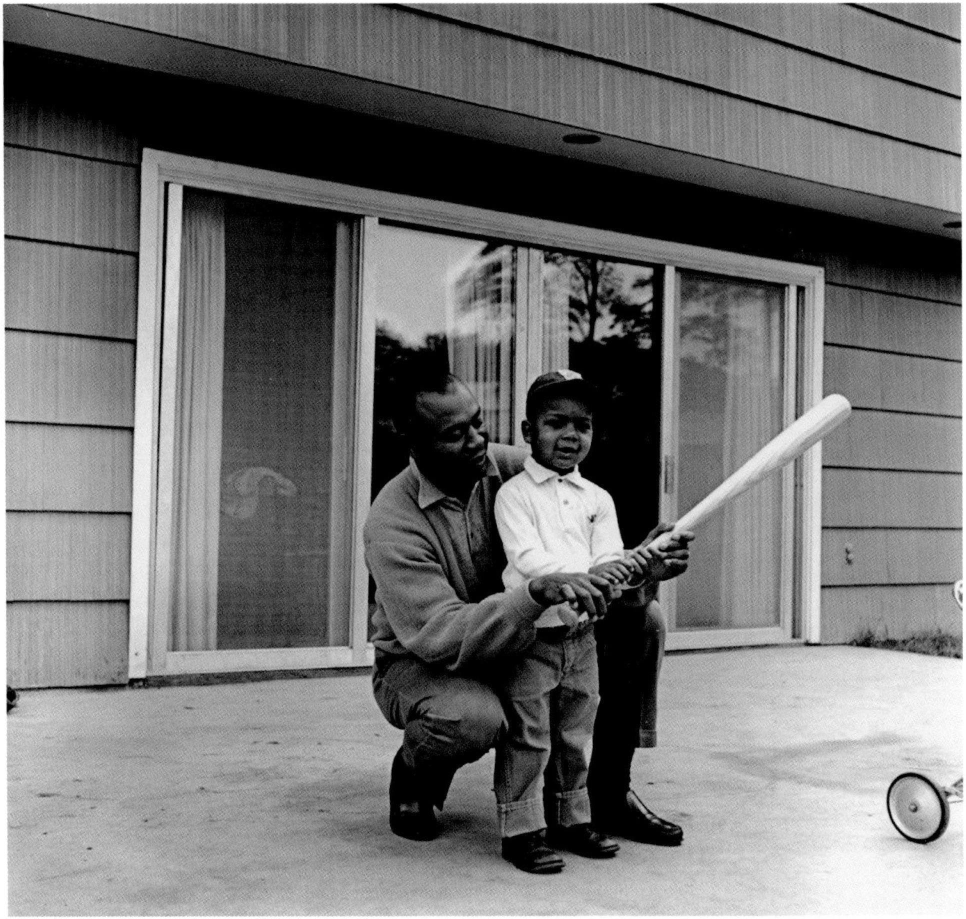

Larry Doby with son Larry Jr., 1960
Moneta Sleet Jr.
—

Larry Doby was the first Black player in the American League. Though an outstanding player, Doby has always been overshadowed by Jackie Robinson who integrated the National League eleven weeks earlier. However, Doby had to endure the same pressures and obstacles that Robinson did without the same level of recognition.

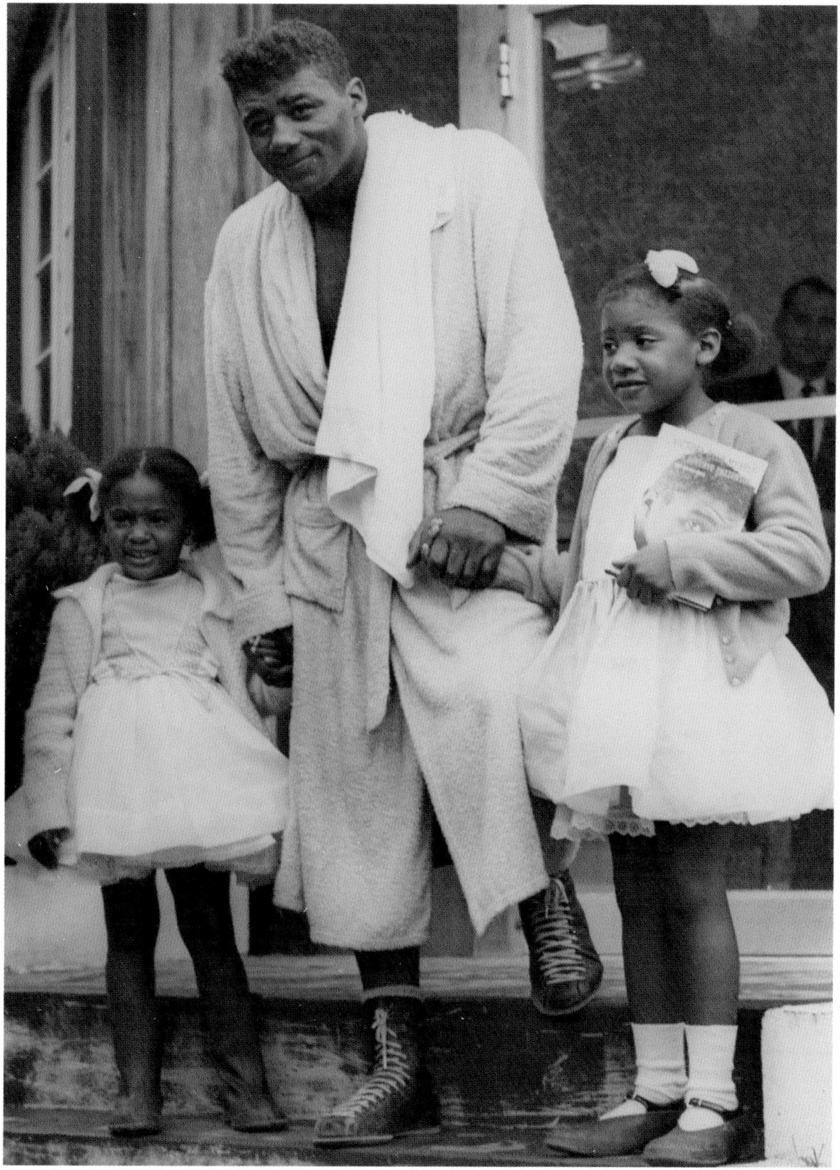

Floyd Patterson with his daughters, July 20, 1962
James Gilbert

—

Heavyweight champion Floyd Patterson is pictured here with his two daughters, Trina and Seneca, just prior to his 1962 title fight against Sonny Liston at Comiskey Park in Chicago. Patterson lost the controversial bout.

Umpire Emmett Ashford makes a call during a Baltimore Orioles vs. New York Yankees game, Baltimore, Maryland,
April 15, 1966
Maurice Sorrell

—

Emmett Ashford was the first Black umpire in Major League Baseball. Because of his talent, enthusiasm, and flair, Ashford became a fan favorite.

"Maybe my style was a little pronounced and unusual, but all I ever asked was to be judged on my competency."

Emmett Ashford

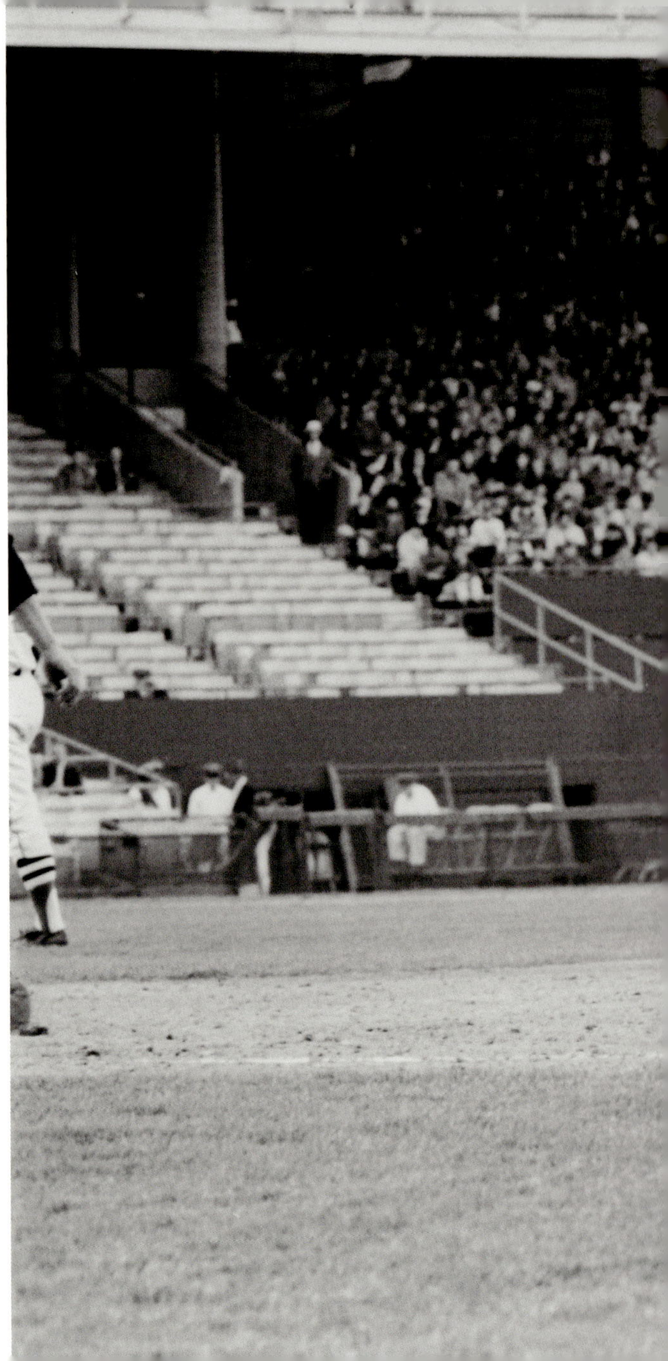

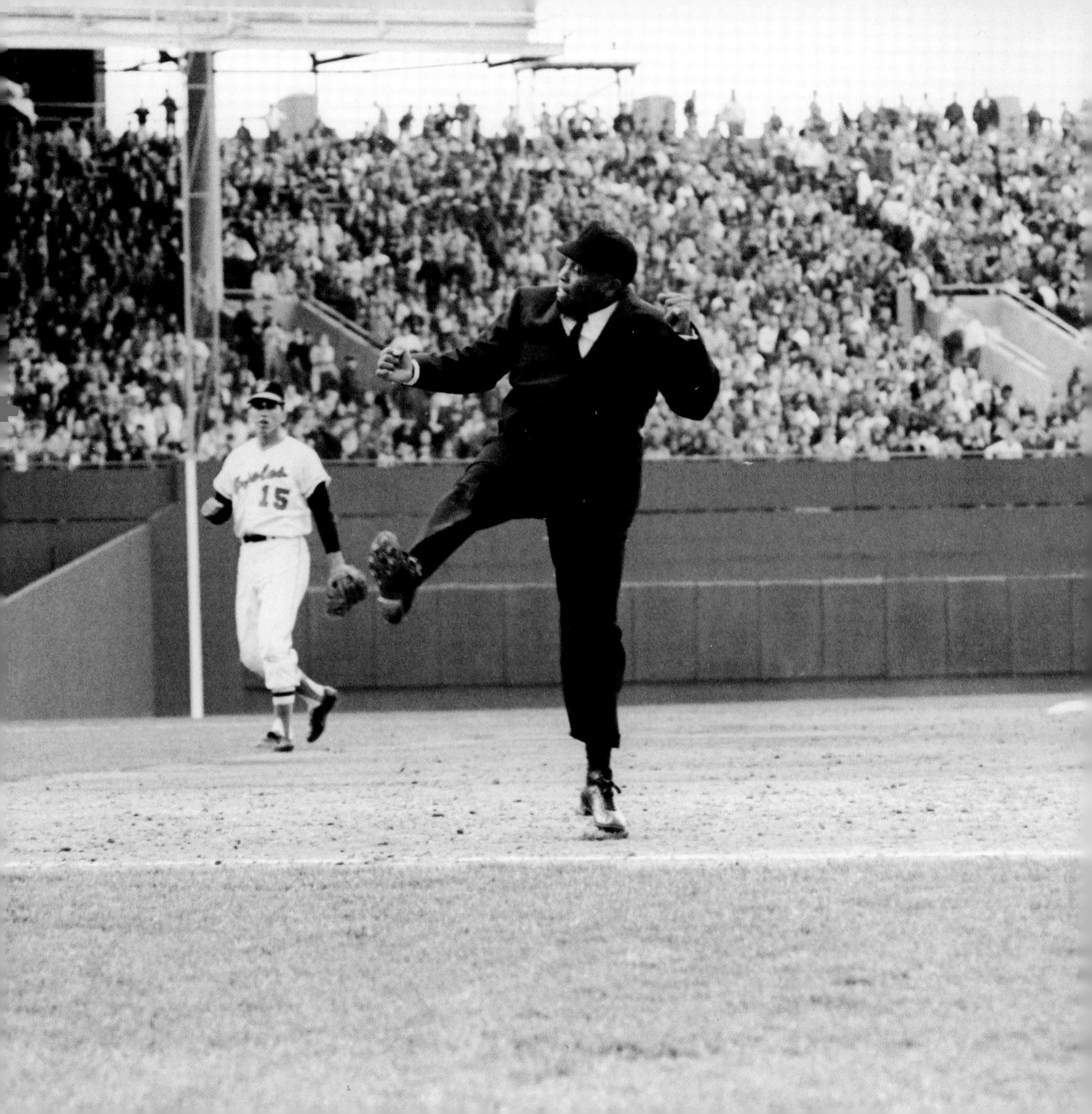
15

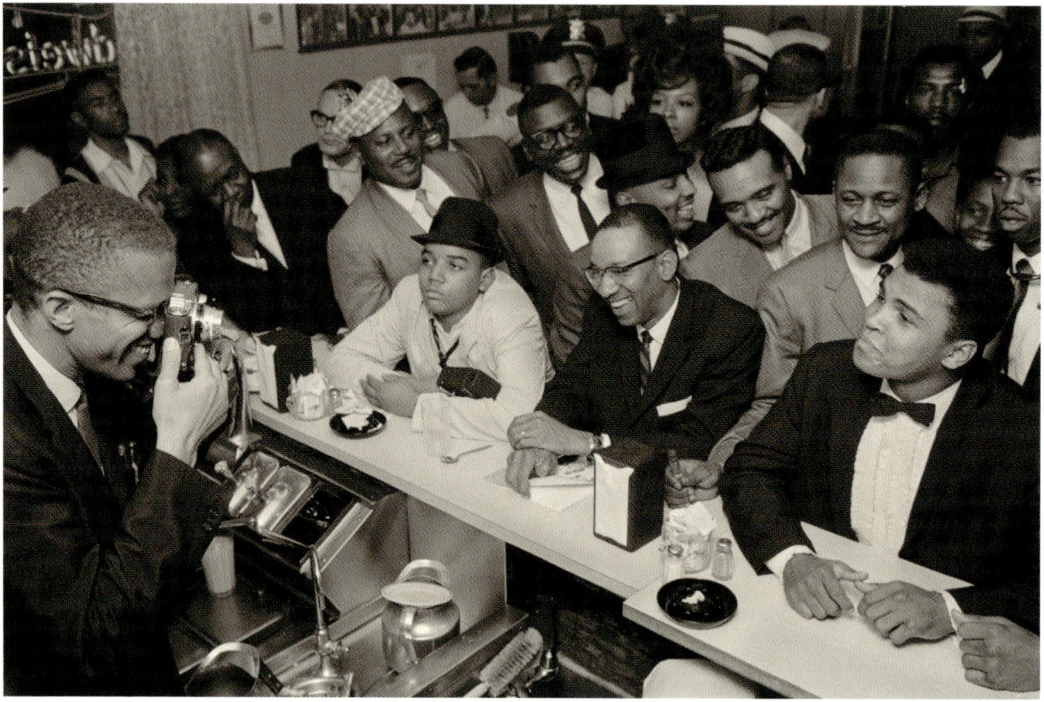

Black Muslim Leader Malcolm X Photographing Cassius Clay, 1964
Bob Gomel
—

Malcom X served as a friend and mentor to Muhammad Ali during the early years of his conversion to Islam.

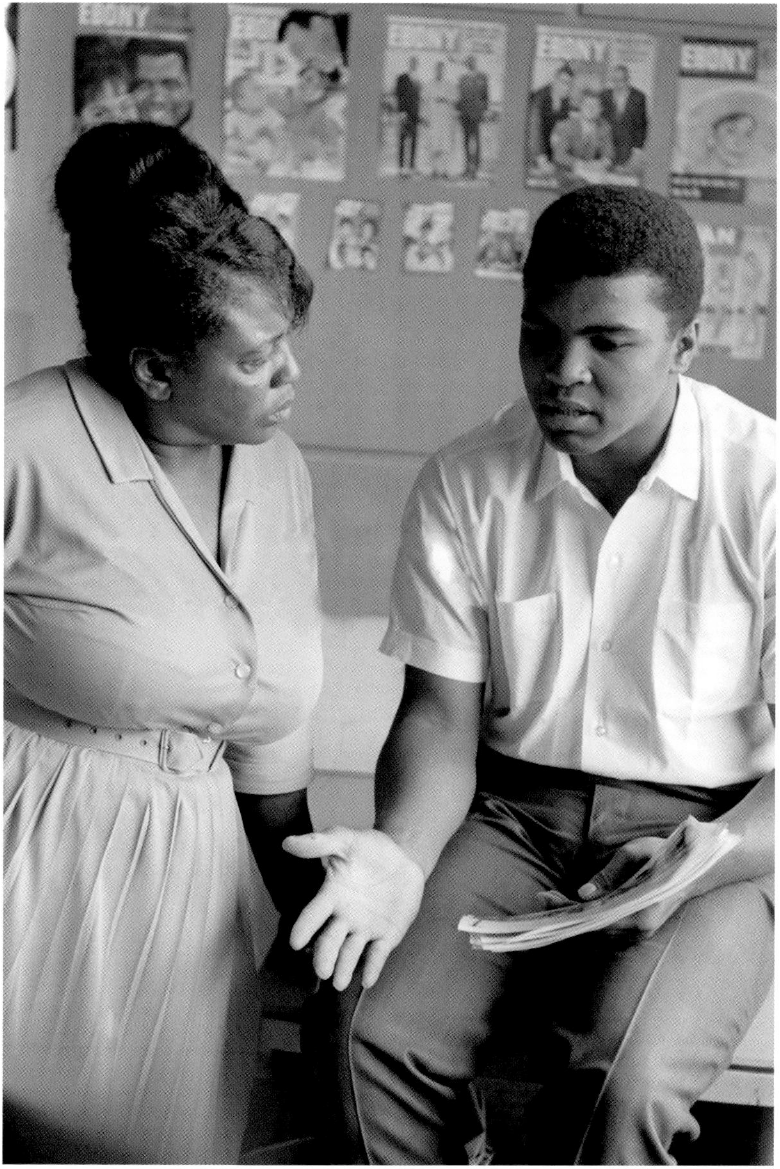

Fannie Lou Hamer and Muhammad Ali talk at Johnson Publishing Company offices, August 1964
Lacey Crawford

—

Voting and civil rights activist Fannie Lou Hamer and Muhammad Ali were frequently featured across Johnson Publishing Company publications such as *Ebony* and *Jet*.

DISRUPTION AND ACCEPTANCE: 1968–1980

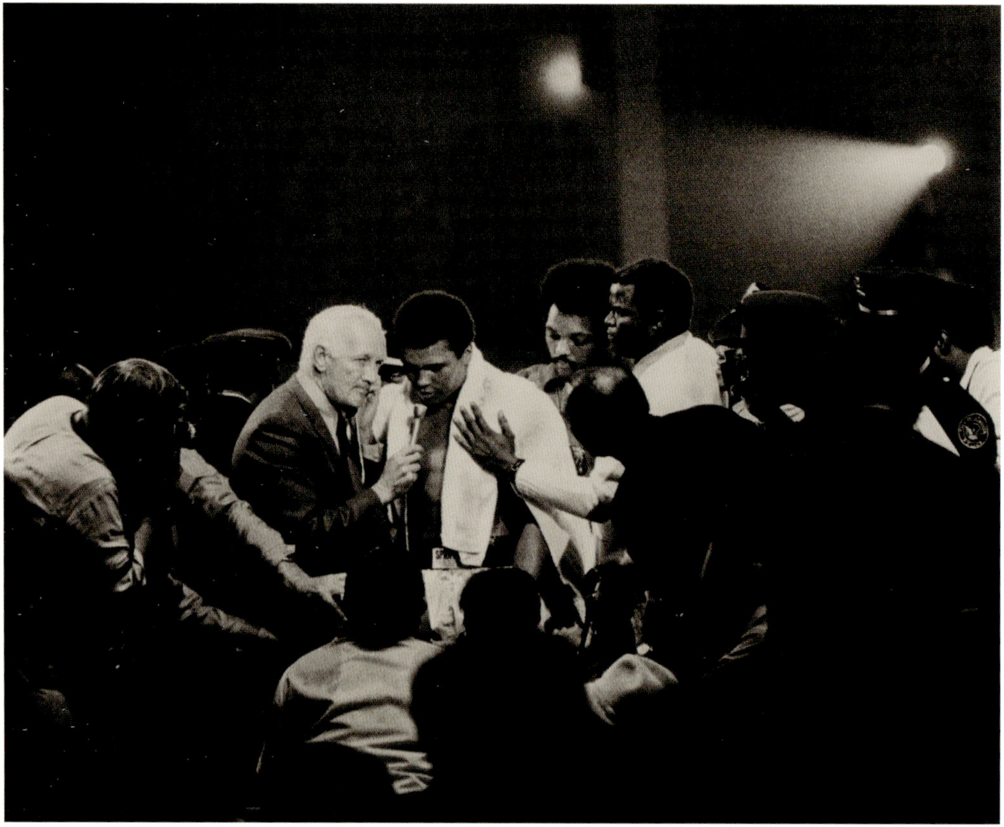

Muhammad Ali "Victory Speech,"
October 26, 1970; printed 2019
Richard Herman
—

Muhammad Ali was suspended from boxing for three and a half years because of his refusal to serve in the military after being drafted during the Vietnam War. His return to the ring was triumphant: he defeated Jerry Quarry in three rounds at Atlanta's Municipal Auditorium in 1970.

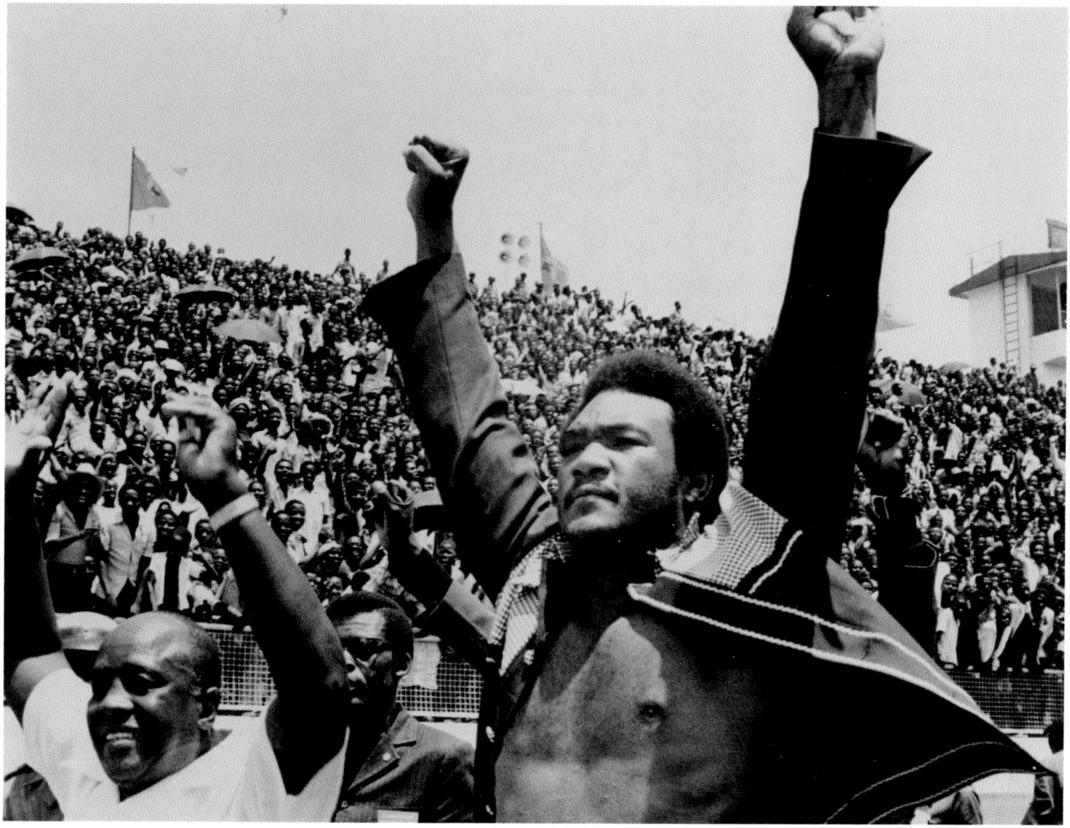

Heavyweight champion George Foreman greets fans before "The Rumble in the Jungle," Zaire, Africa, October 1974
Unidentified photographer

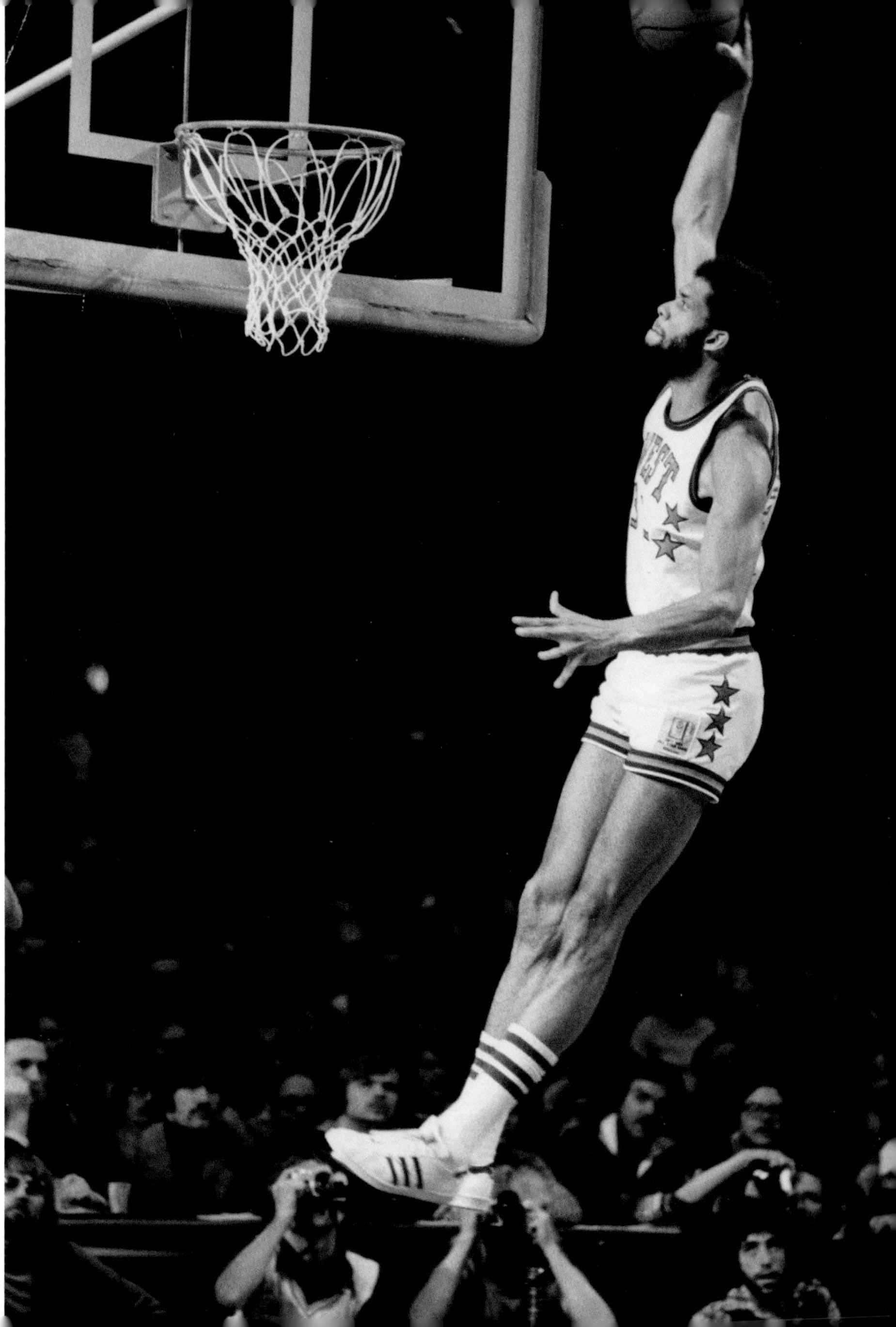

Kareem Abdul-Jabbar executing a slam dunk during the NBA East–West All-Star Game, 1978
Ozier Muhammad

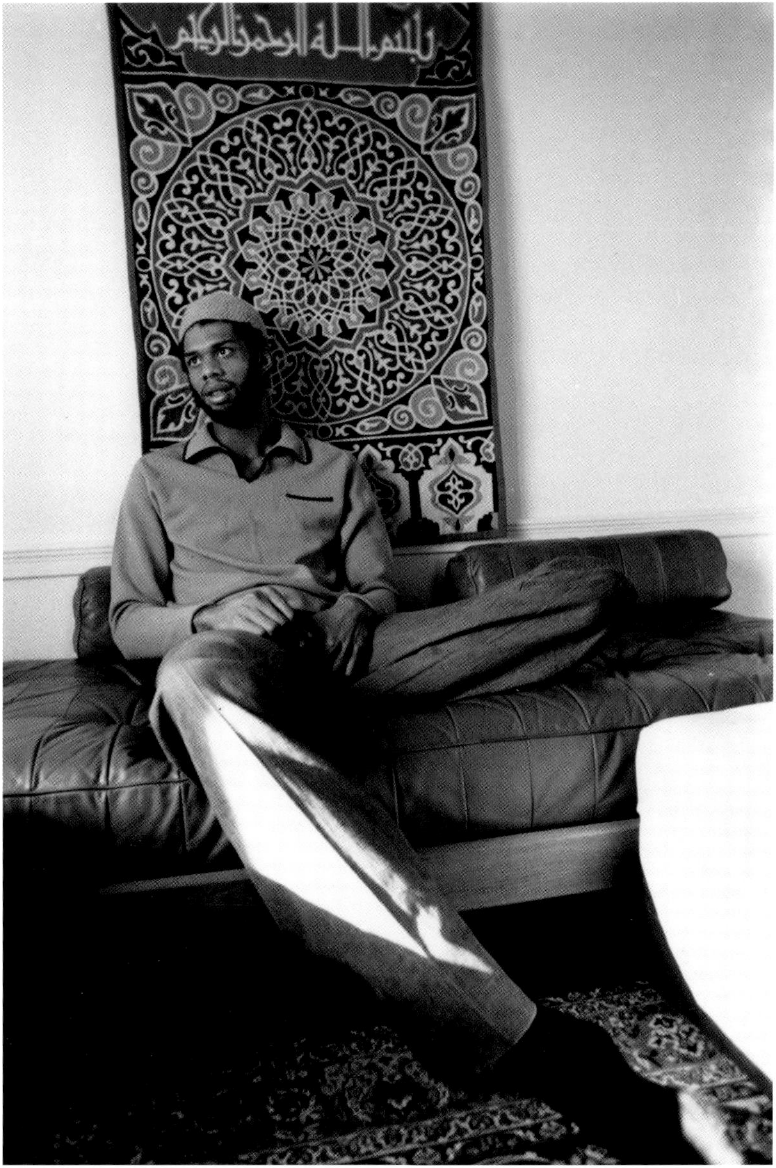

Kareem Abdul-Jabbar at home, Milwaukee, Wisconsin, 1975
Ozier Muhammad

—

In 1971 at the age of twenty-four, Lew Alcindor converted to Islam and took the name Kareem Abdul-Jabbar.

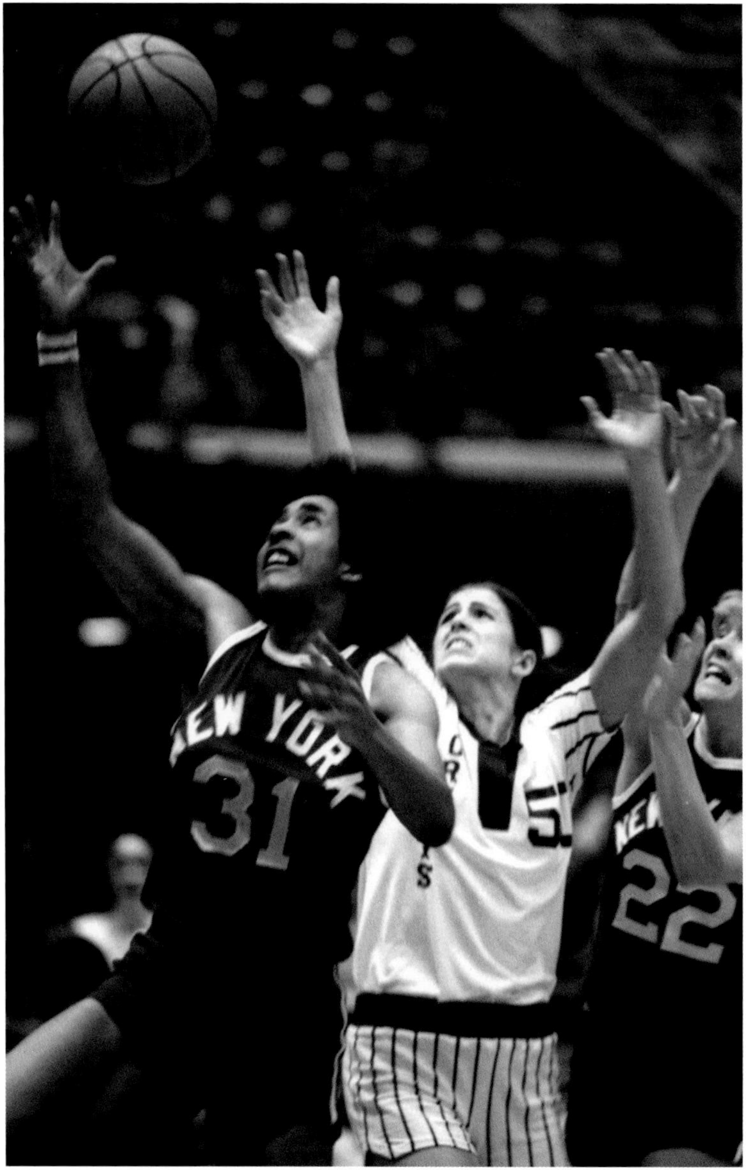

Althea Gwyn, New York Stars vs. Iowa Cornets, Women's Professional Basketball League, 1978–80
David Peterson

—

The Women's Professional Basketball League, in existence from 1978 until 1981, included outstanding players representing many of the major cities in the United States. The league hoped to take advantage of increased opportunities for women to compete in sports after the passage of Title IX in 1972.

Debra Kay Thomas, Iowa Cornets, Women's Professional Basketball League, 1978–80
David Peterson

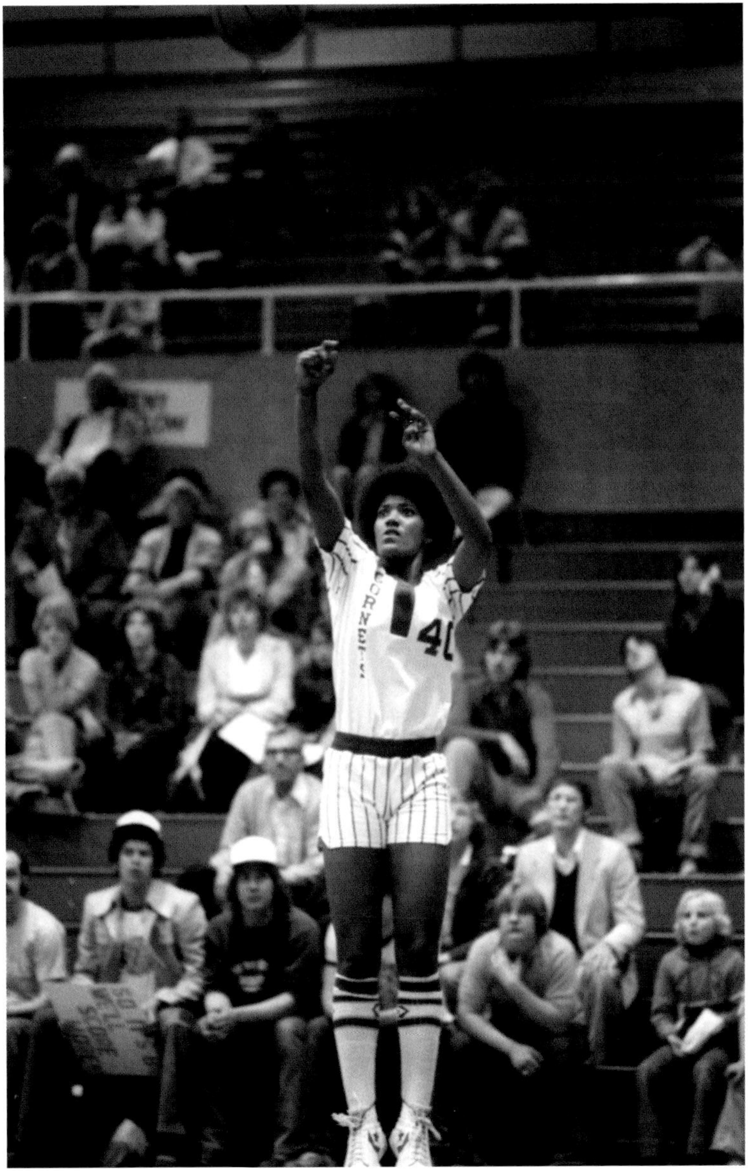

Curt Flood answering questions during a news conference, 1970
Maurice Sorrell

—

Curt Flood was an all-star baseball player, but he is best known for filing a lawsuit against Major League Baseball for violating anti-trust laws that reached the U.S. Supreme Court. Flood's lawsuit was unsuccessful, but it galvanized professional baseball players to continue his efforts. Five years later, the reserve clause was eliminated, and free agency started, which led to higher salaries for players.

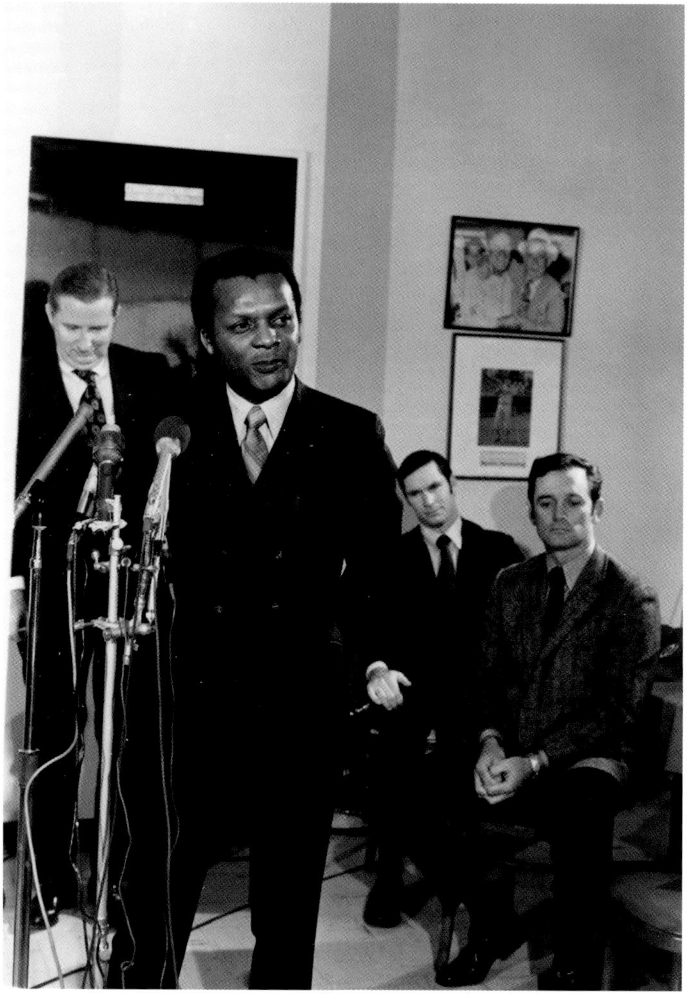

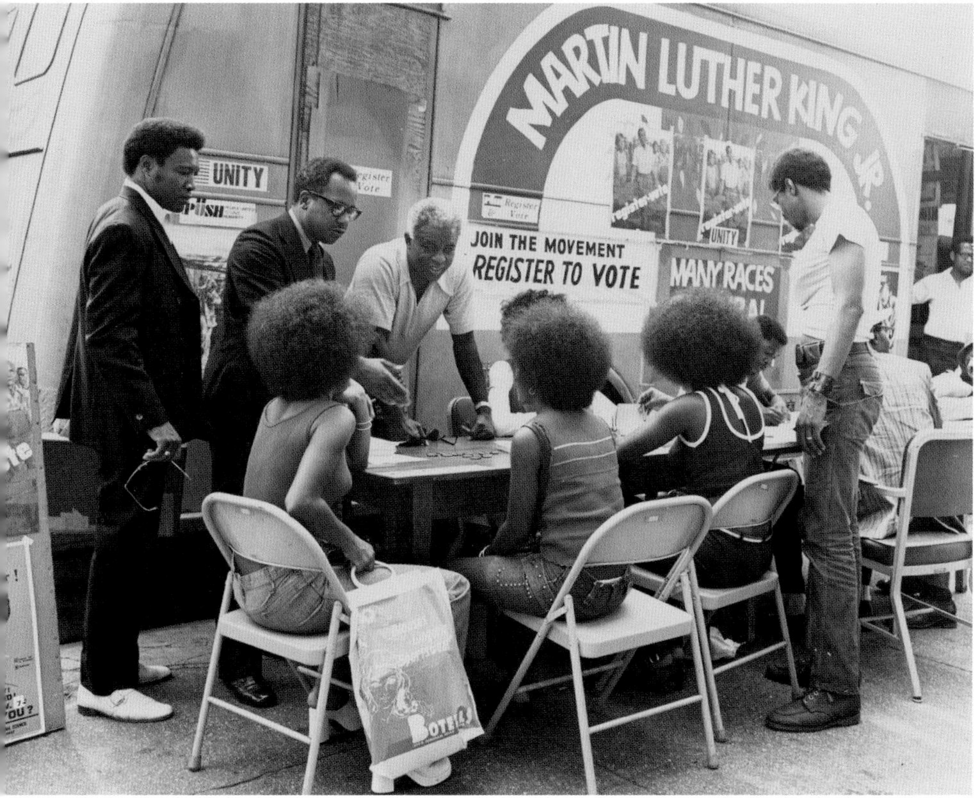

Jackie Robinson at a voter registration event, 1972
J. Alan Fisher

—

Jackie Robinson (leaning on table) was very active in politics both in his playing days and in his post-baseball career. One of the issues about which he was most passionate was voting rights.

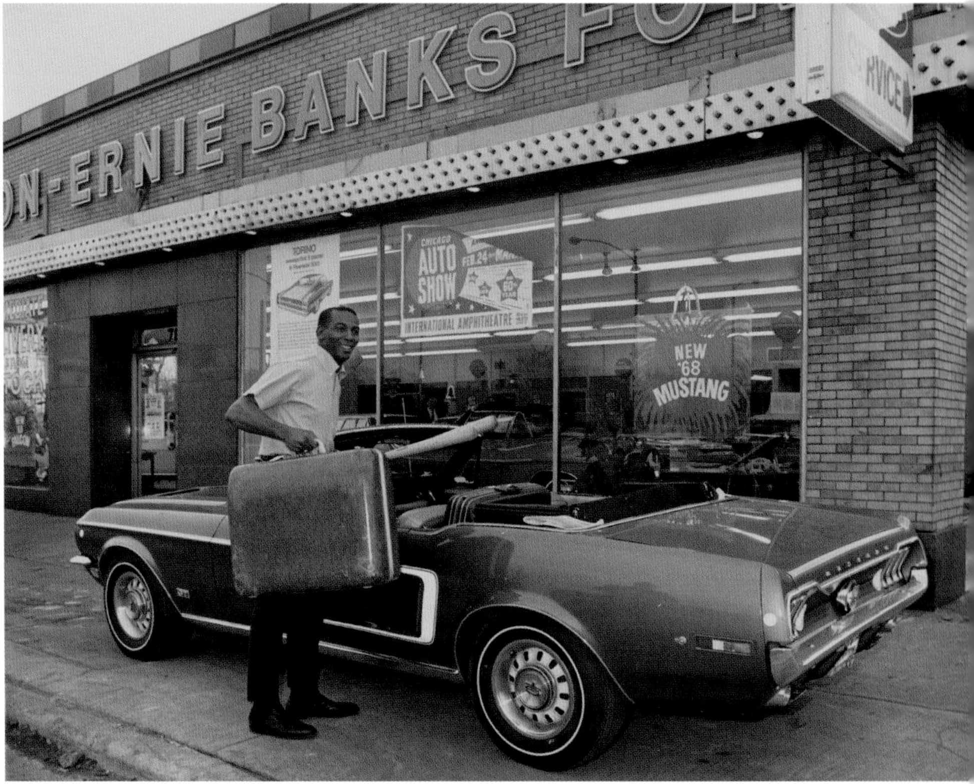

Ernie Banks outside his car dealership, Chicago, 1968
New Amsterdam News
—
Ernie Banks, long-time Chicago Cubs shortstop and one of the most beloved figures in the history of baseball, parlayed his exploits on the playing field into success in the world of business. One example of this success was his Ford Motor Company car dealership on Chicago's South Side.

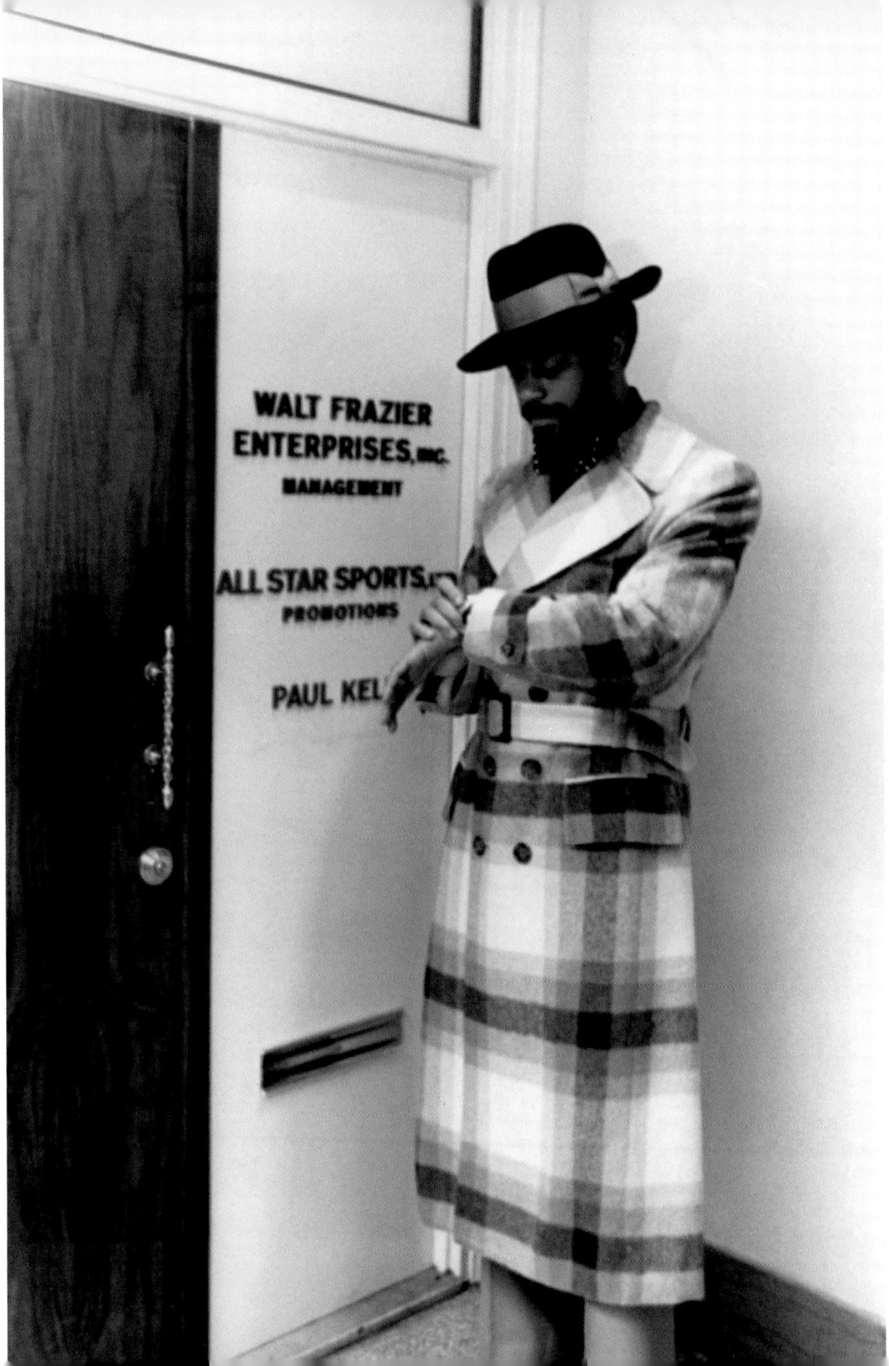

Walt Frazier outside the offices of Walt Frazier Enterprises, New York City, 1974
Moneta Sleet Jr.

—

Walt Frazier, all-star New York Knicks guard, stands outside his New York City management firm dressed in the fashionable style that marked his career. Frazier was among a growing cohort of athletes who used their athletic fame to establish business ventures.

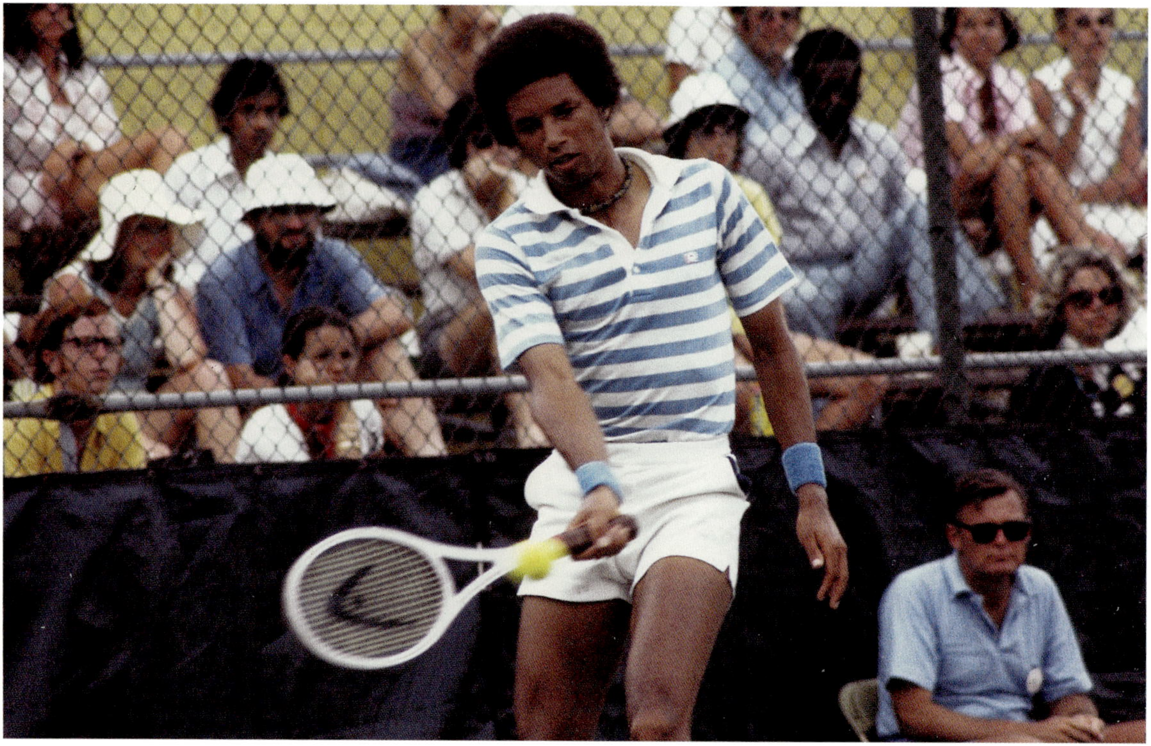

Arthur Ashe during the Washington Star International Tennis Tournament, Washington, D.C., July 1975
Maurice Sorrell
—

Arthur Ashe fashioned an outstanding career on and off the tennis court. A winner of three major titles (1968 U.S. Open, 1970 Australian Open, and 1975 Wimbledon Championship), he dedicated his life to advocating for human rights.

Lee Elder at the Masters Tournament, Augusta, Georgia, April 1975
Moneta Sleet Jr.

—

Lee Elder made history in 1975 when he became the first African American to play in the prestigious Masters Tournament at the Augusta National Golf Club in Augusta, Georgia. Though he failed to advance beyond the second round, Elder would go on to play in the legendary tournament five more times, making the cut in three of them, and win several Professional Golfers' Association (PGA) sponsored titles.

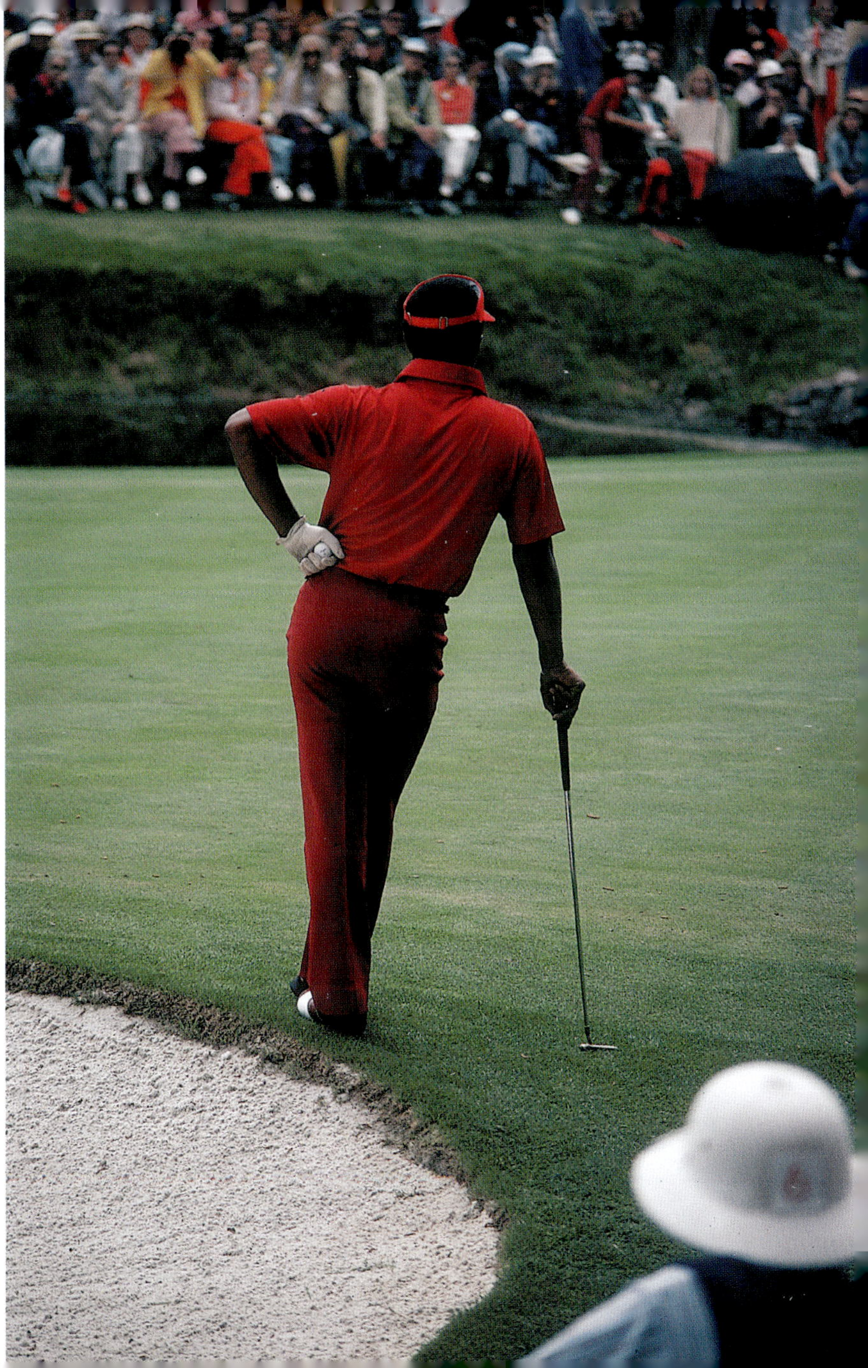

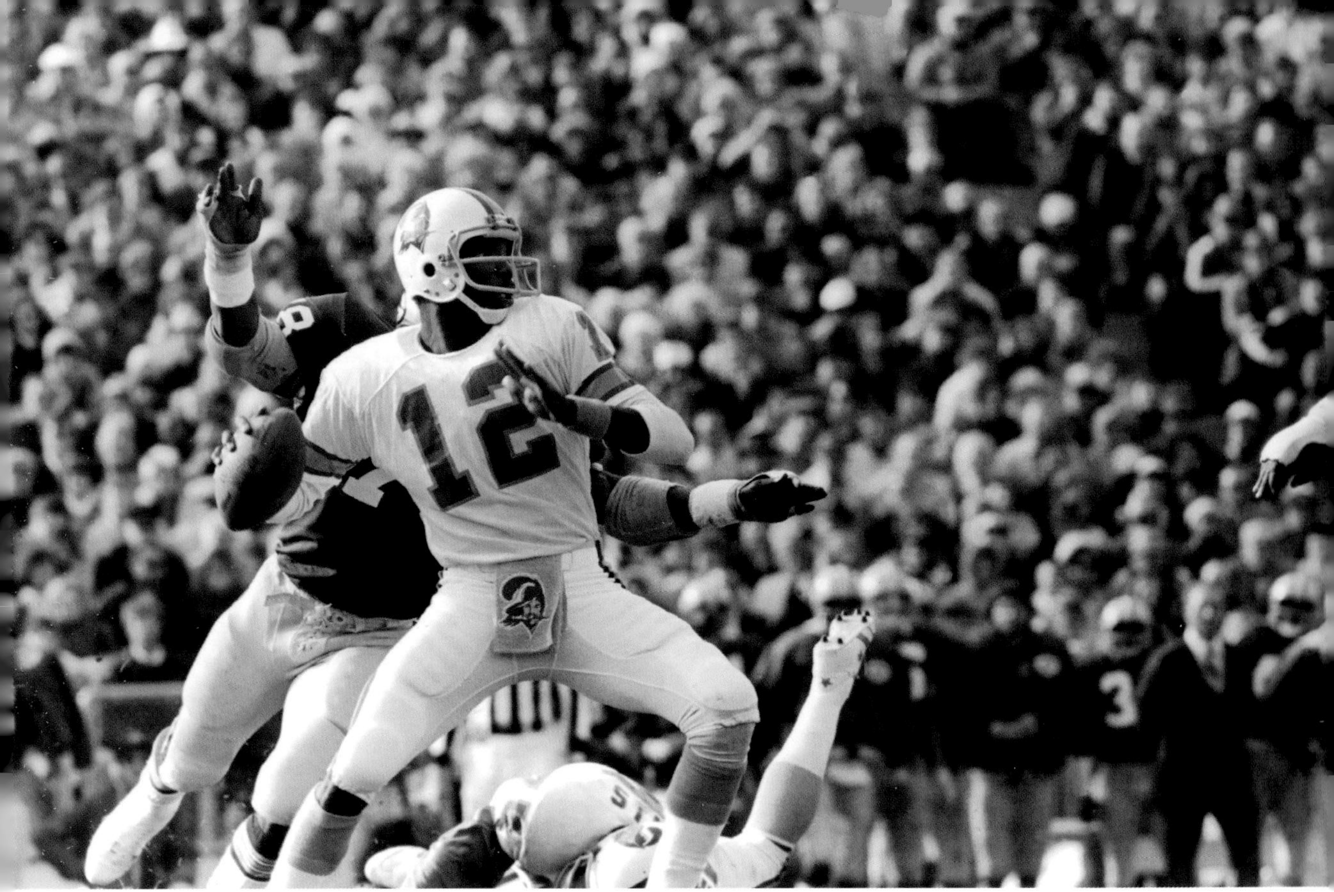

Doug Williams, Tampa Bay Buccaneers vs. Green Bay Packers, Green Bay, Wisconsin, October 29, 1978
Vandell Cobb
—

Quarterback Doug Williams, pictured here in his rookie season in the National Football League with the Tampa Bay Buccaneers, made history when he led Washington to a Super Bowl victory in 1988. His success demonstrated that African Americans could succeed at the game's most important position.

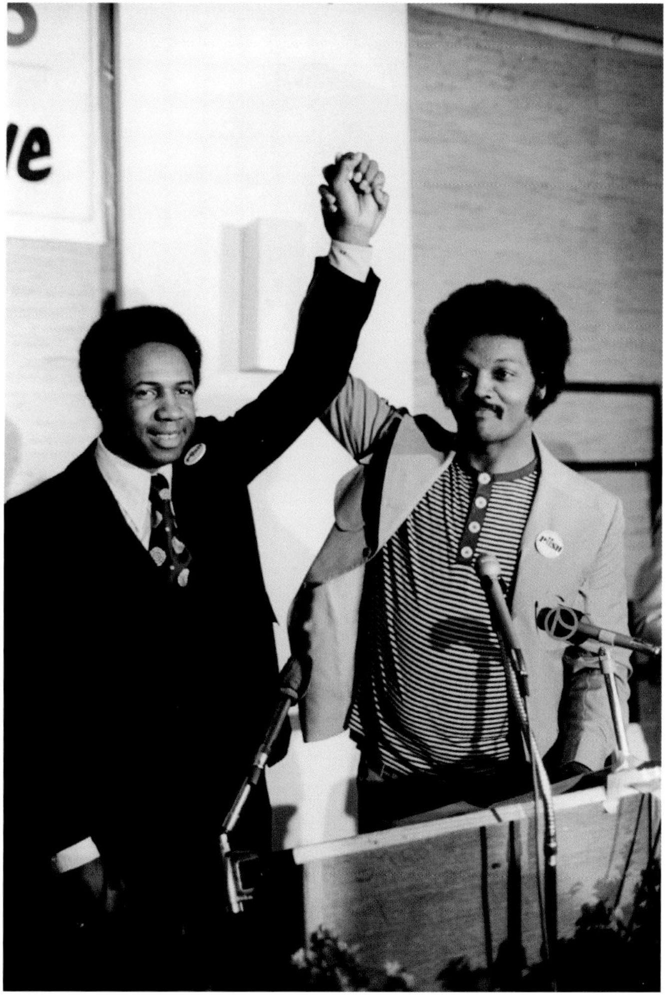

Jesse Jackson celebrates with Frank Robinson, 1975
Ozier Muhammad

—

In 1975 Frank Robinson made history as the first Black manager in Major League Baseball when he signed a contract with Cleveland. Reverend Jesse Jackson and many others enthusiastically celebrated this historic event.

INNOVATION AND DOMINANCE: 1980–TODAY

John Thompson leans on a stack of books, 1984
Maurice Sorrell

—

Georgetown University basketball coach John Thompson was a strong advocate for increased access to higher education for African American athletes.

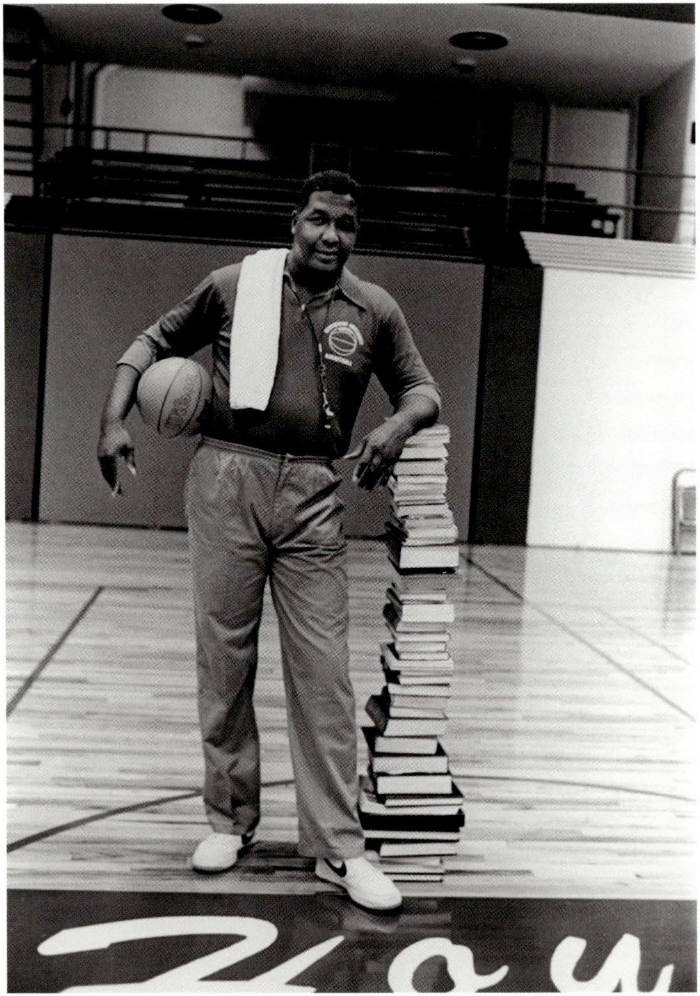

Earvin "Magic" Johnson teams with Shaquille O'Neal, 1992
Ken Coleman

—

Magic Johnson (left) and Shaquille O'Neal (right) competed in the 1992 "Midsummer Night's Magic" benefit basketball game. This event, hosted by Magic Johnson, was at one point the second-highest-grossing fundraiser for the United Negro College Fund.

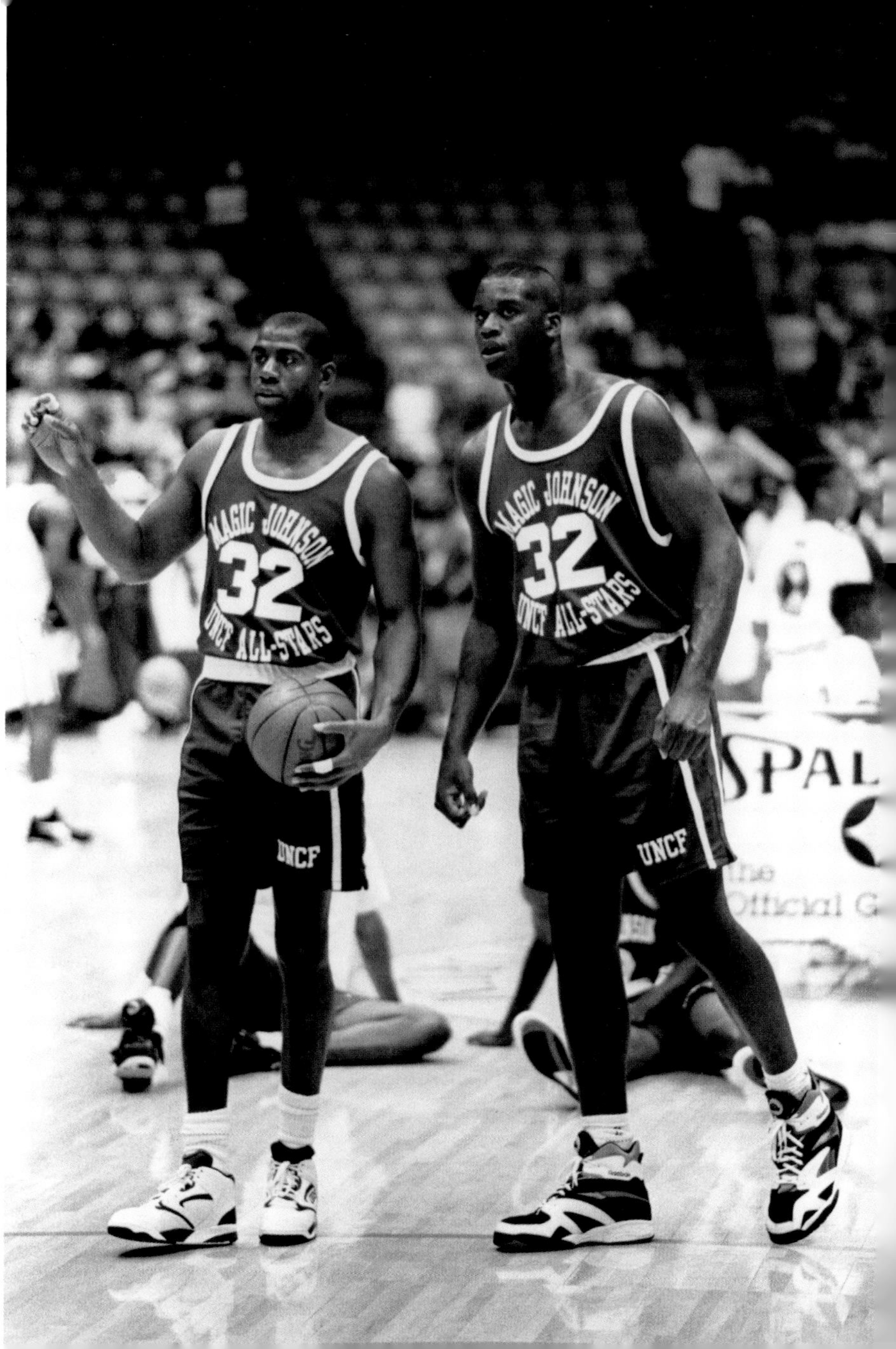

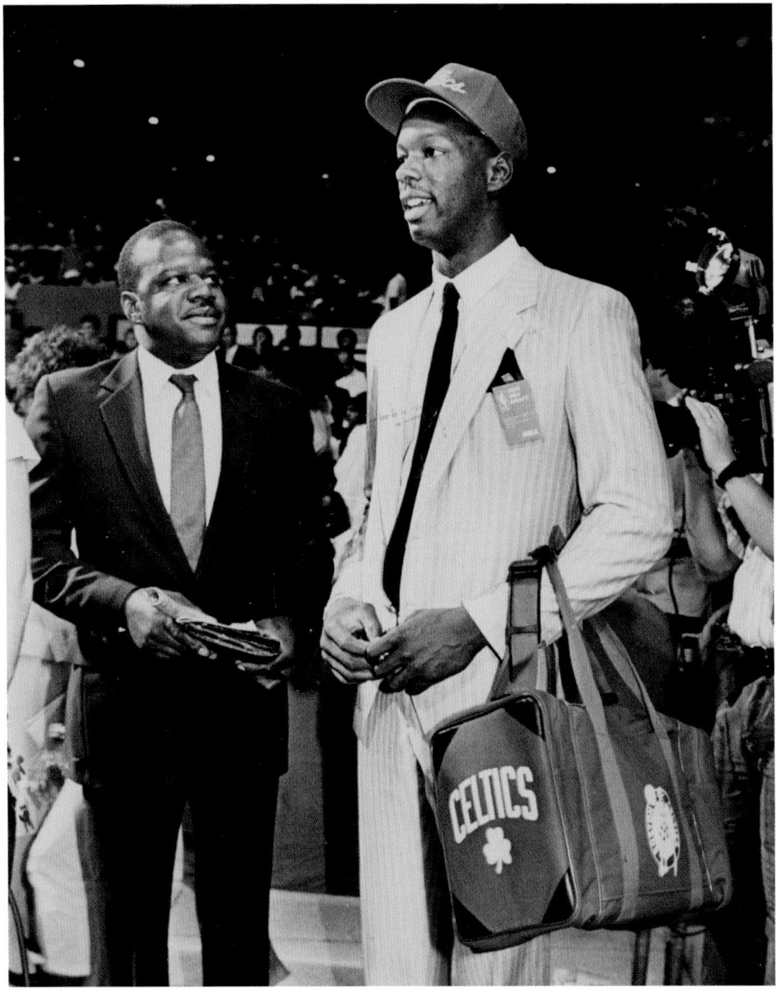

Len Bias with his dad, James Bias Jr., on NBA Draft Night, 1986
Jim Mahoney

—

Len Bias, a small forward from the University of Maryland, was chosen by the Boston Celtics as the second pick in the 1986 NBA draft. Unfortunately, tragedy struck shortly after he was drafted when he died of a drug overdose in his college dormitory room.

Michael Jordan, 1989
Vandell Cobb

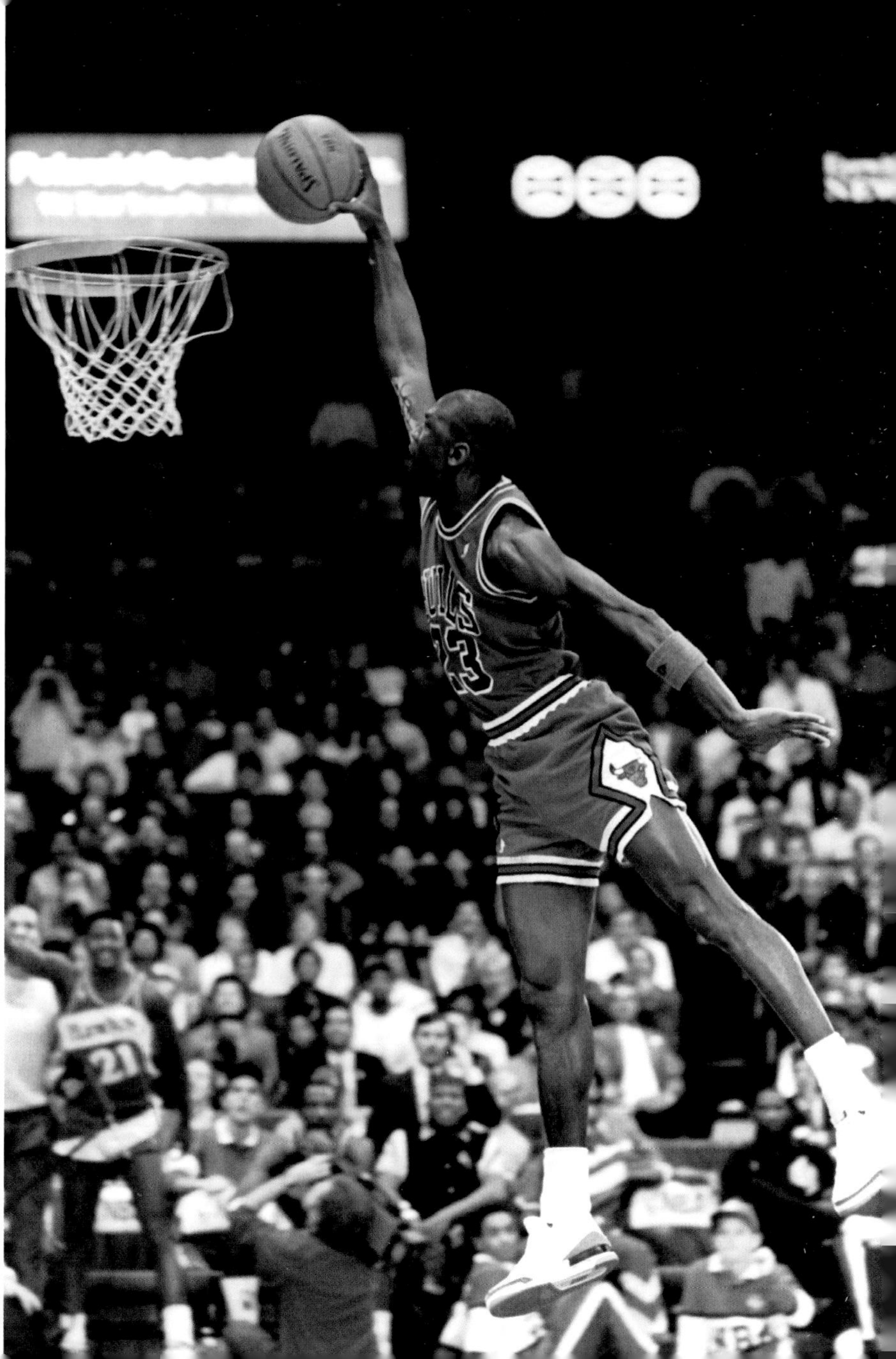

Carl Lewis competing in the long jump for Willingboro High School during the South Jersey Sectionals tournament, May 26, 1979; printed 1984
Dennis McDonald

—

Carl Lewis is one of track and field's most decorated athletes. In the 1984 Olympic Games in Los Angeles, he memorably captured four gold medals in the same events (100 meters, 200 meters, 4 × 100 meters relay, and long jump) as had legendary Olympian Jesse Owens nearly fifty years earlier in Berlin.

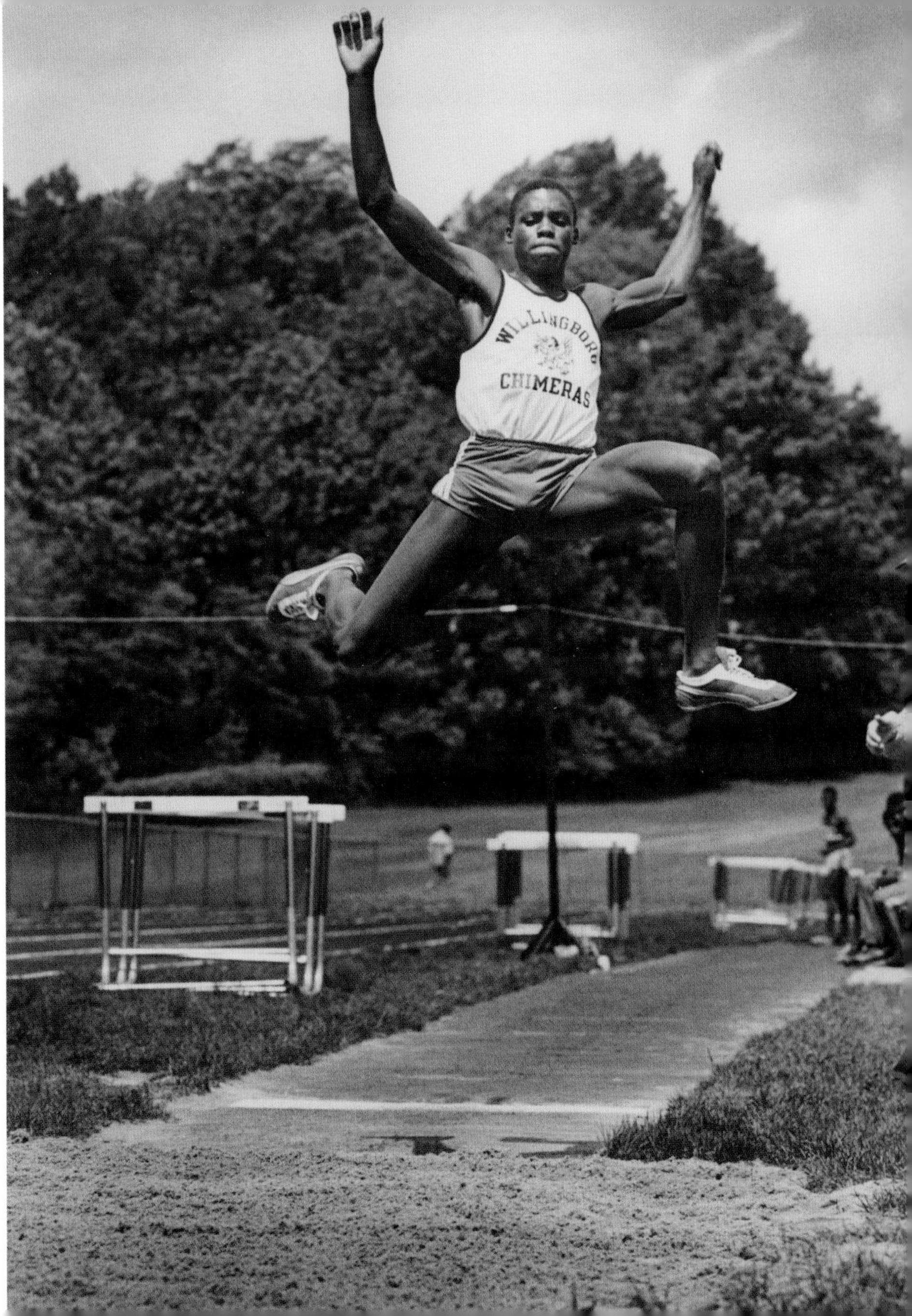

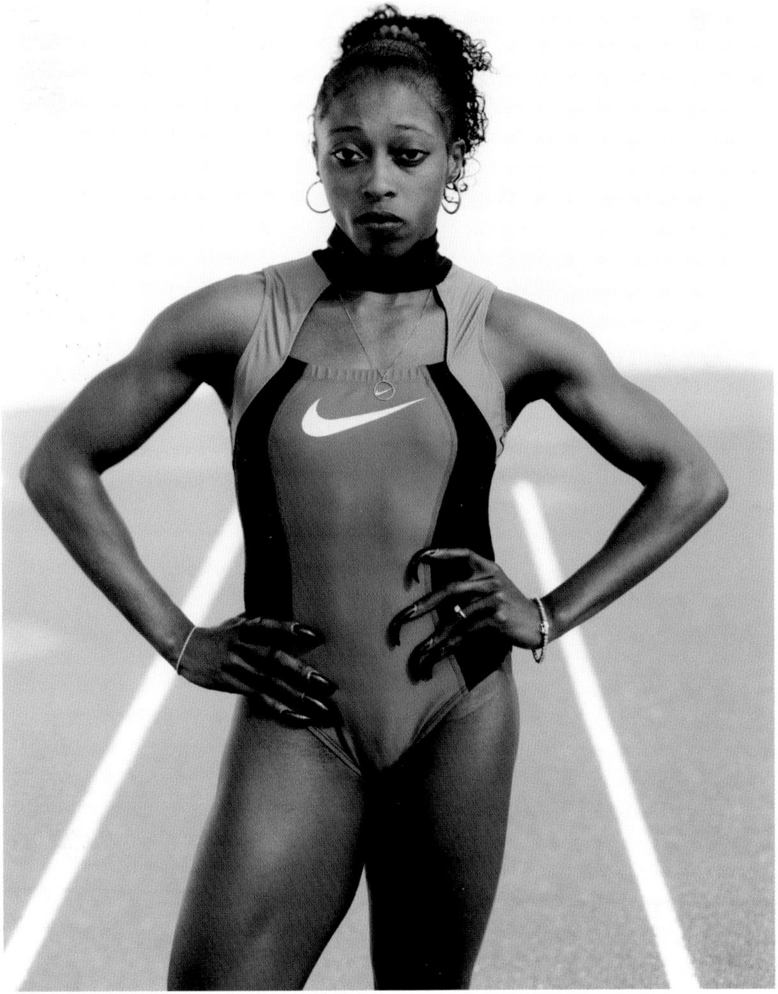

Gail Devers, Los Angeles, California, 1996
Walter Iooss Jr.

—

Track star Gail Devers overcame debilitating illnesses, including Graves' disease, to fashion an outstanding Olympic career. Among her many triumphs were gold medals in the 100 meters at the Summer Olympics in Barcelona in 1992 and in Atlanta in 1996.

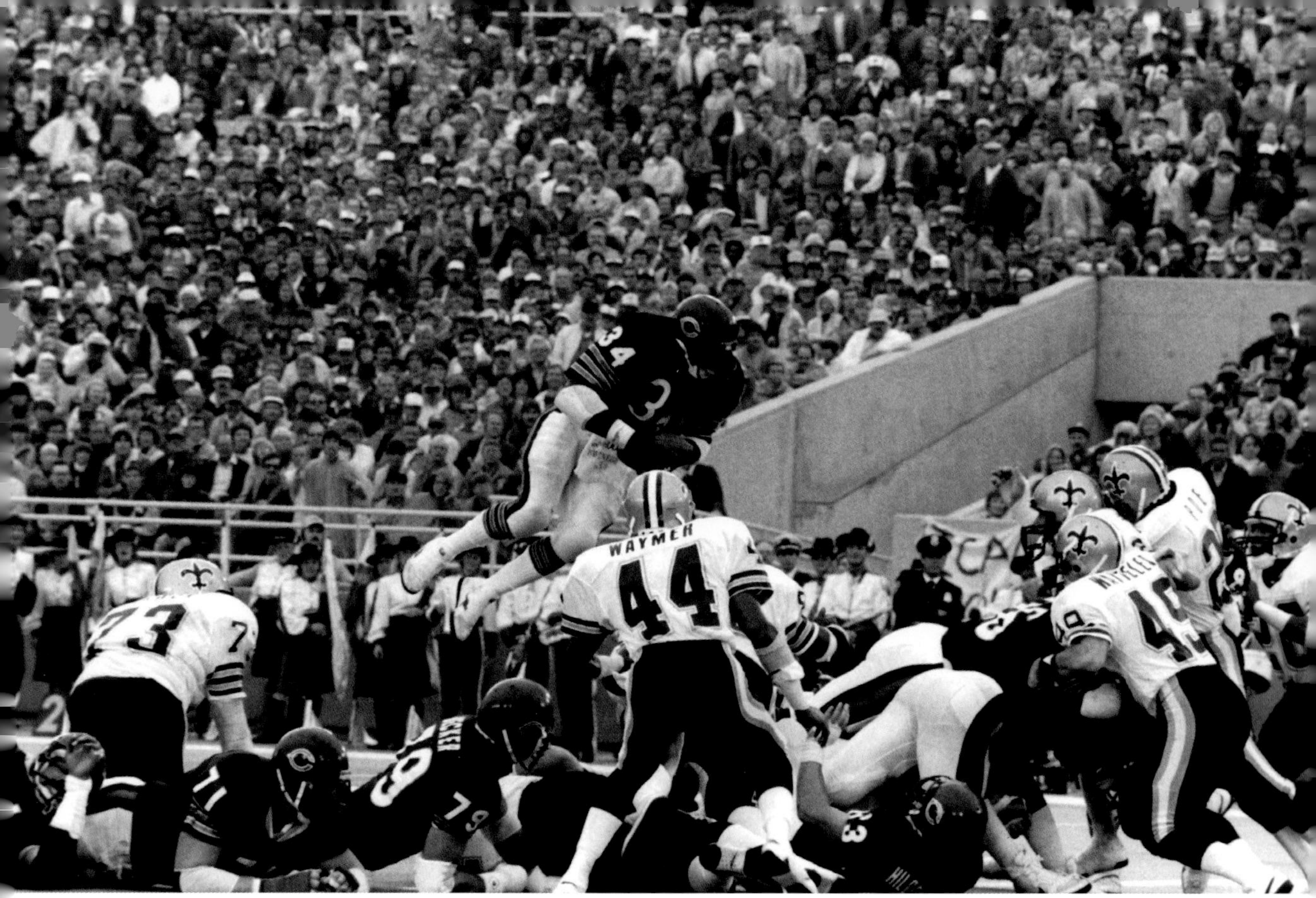

Walter Payton, Chicago Bears vs. New Orleans Saints, Chicago, Illinois, September 2, 1984
Vandell Cobb
—

Known as "Sweetness," Walter Payton rushed for at least 1,200 yards in ten of the thirteen years he played for the Chicago Bears. He had a unique running style that included leaping over the top of would-be tacklers.

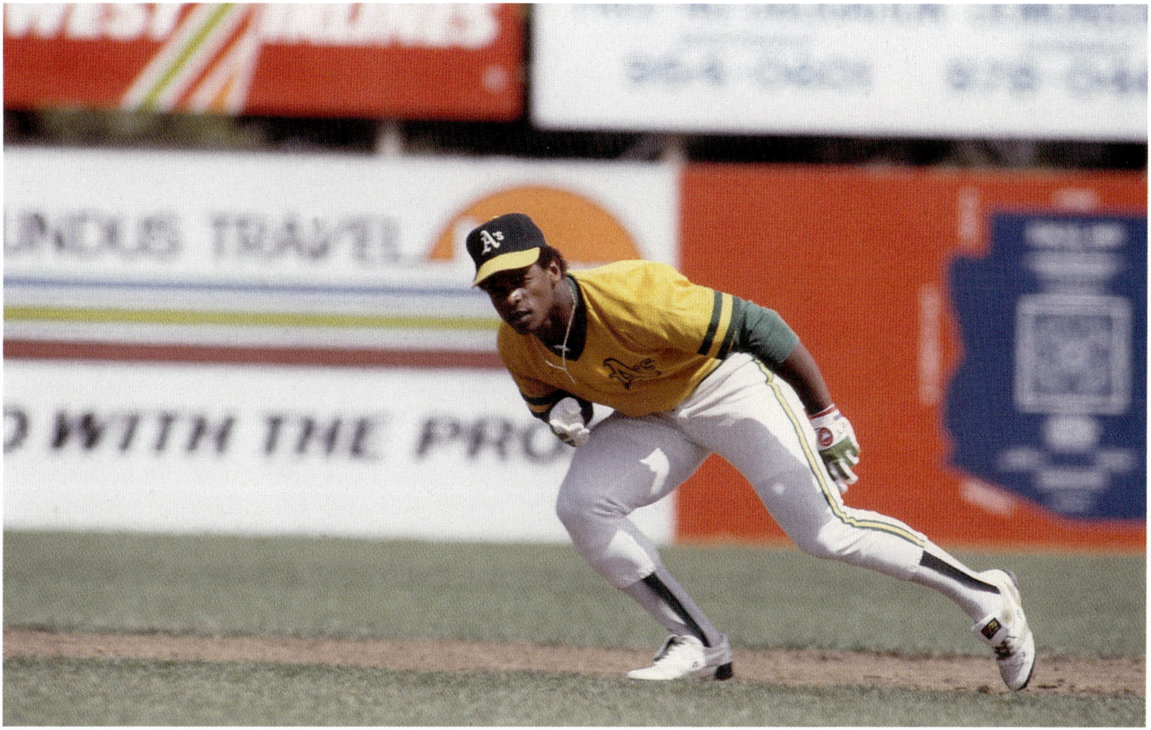

Rickey Henderson,
1983
Vandell Cobb
—

Rickey Henderson, nicknamed the "Man of Steal," is widely considered the greatest leadoff hitter in baseball.

In twenty-five years in Major League Baseball, he accumulated 3,055 hits and a remarkable 1,406 stolen bases.

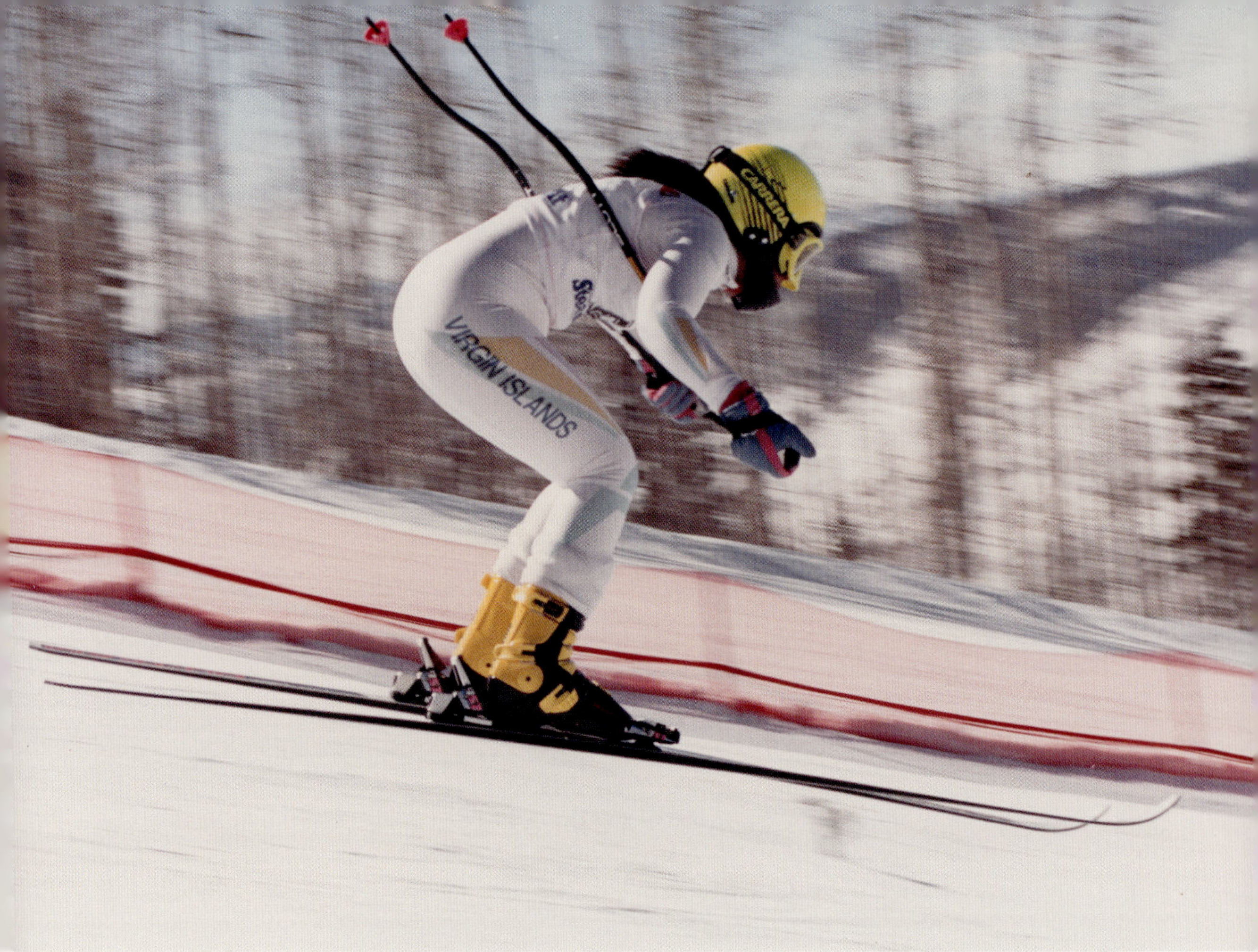

Seba Johnson during the 1989 Alpine Skiing World Cup, Steamboat Springs, Colorado, February 1989
Margaret Chidlaw
—

Seba Johnson was born in the United States Virgin Islands but raised in Stateline, Nevada. She was the first Black woman to compete in Alpine skiing at the Winter Olympics. She participated in the slalom events when she was fourteen in Calgary, Canada, in 1988, and in Albertville, France, in 1992.

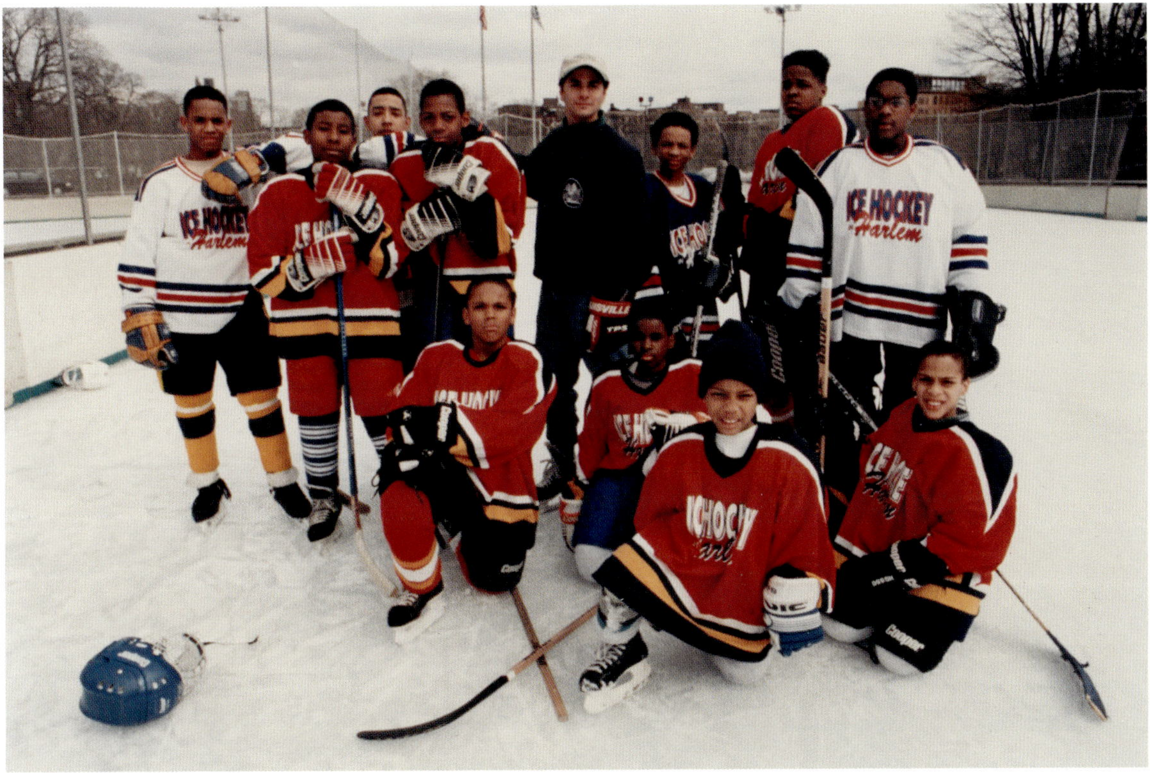

Ice Hockey in Harlem team and coach, after 1987
Unidentified photographer
—

Founded in 1987, Ice Hockey in Harlem is a youth sport organization devoted to teaching the sport while also developing life skills among its participants.

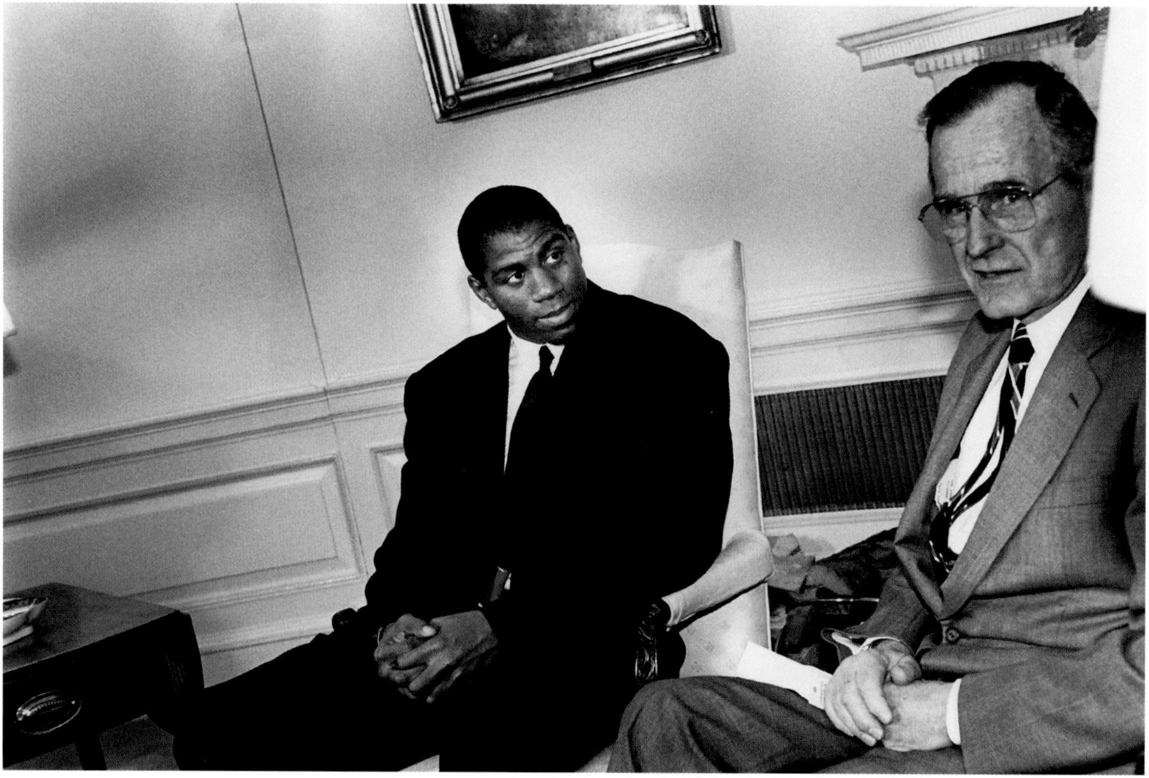

Magic Johnson with President George H.W. Bush, 1992
Maurice Sorrell
—

In November 1991, President George H.W. Bush appointed Magic Johnson to his National Commission on AIDS shortly after the basketball star announced he had tested positive for HIV. Depicted here during his first meeting with the president at the White House, Johnson urged Bush to be more involved in the work of the Commission.

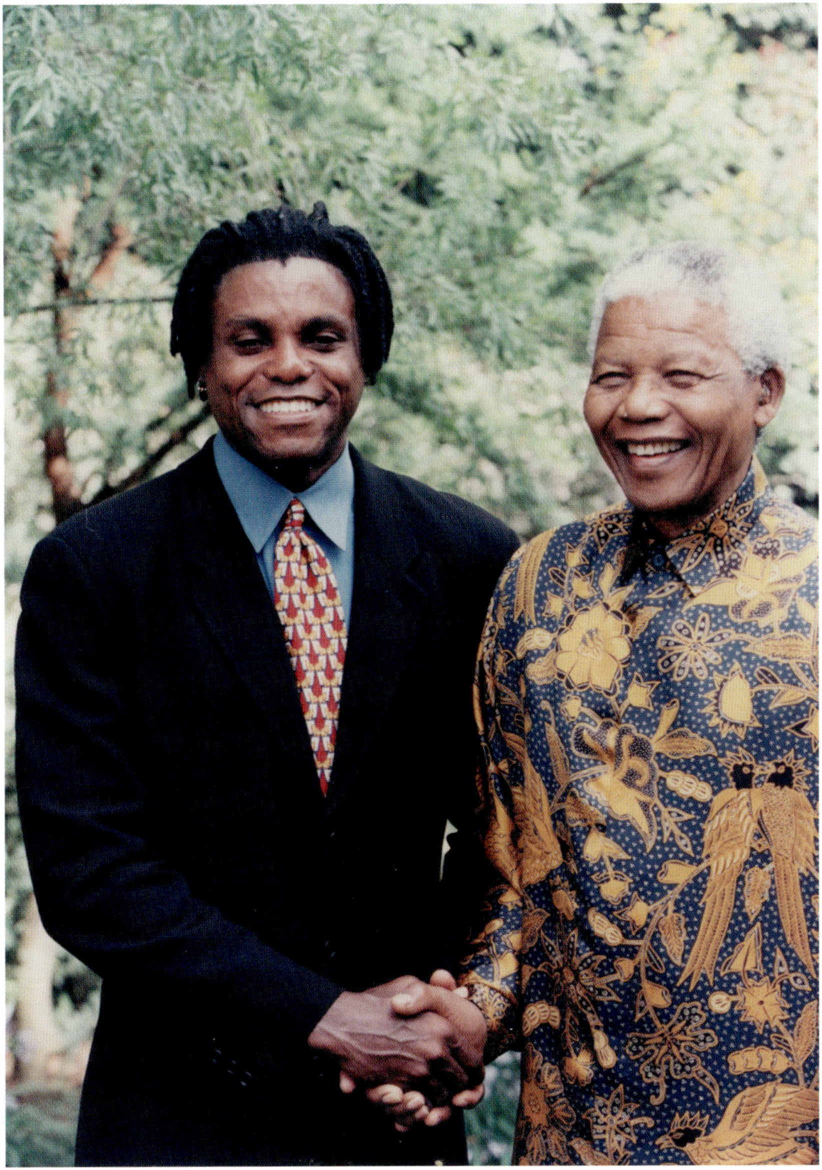

Carl Lewis and Nelson Mandela, 1997
Wessel Oosthuiza

—

South African President Nelson Mandela, an amateur boxer, believed in the ability of sports to bridge racial divides, evidenced during the Rugby World Cup in 1995. As a gesture of unity he famously donned a green and gold jersey of the South African national team, the Springboks, which had come to symbolize white supremacy.

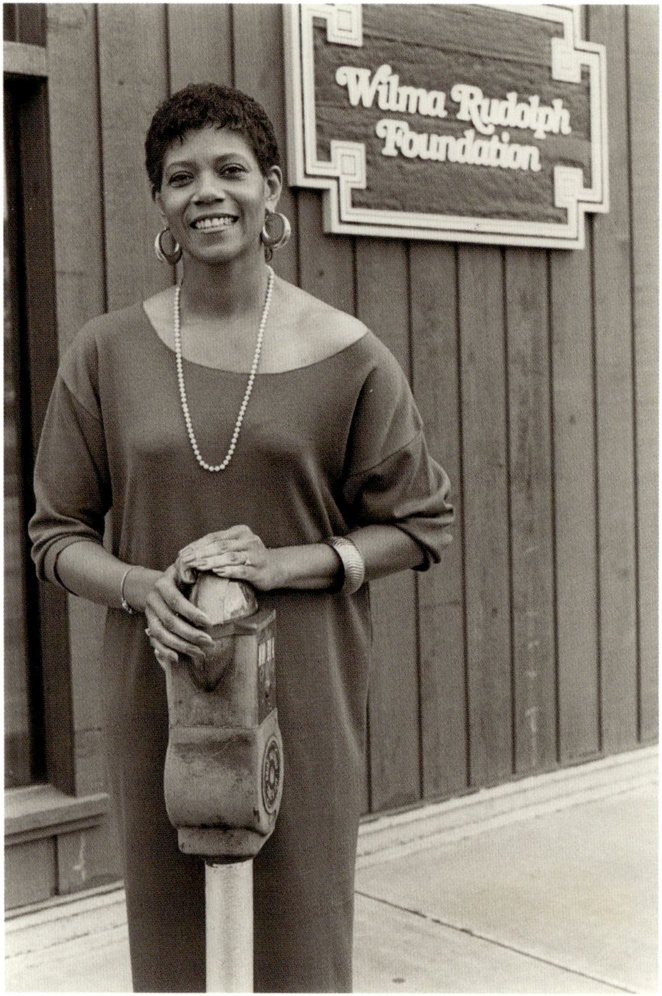

Wilma Rudolph in front of the Wilma Rudolph Foundation headquarters, Indianapolis, Indiana, 1984
James L. Mitchell

—

In 1984, Wilma Rudolph, three-time gold medalist in the 1960 Rome Olympics, started her foundation, which worked to promote community-based, youth-oriented athletic and academic programs.

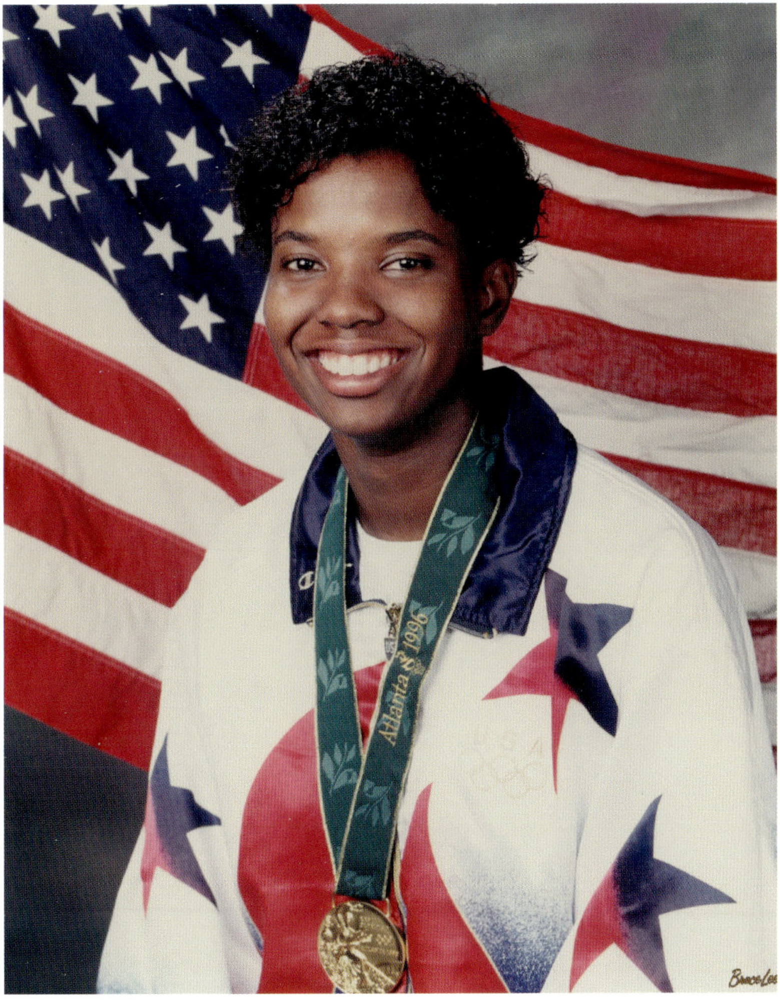

Briana Scurry wearing an Olympic gold medal, 1996
Bruce Lee Photography

—

Briana Scurry is considered one of the greatest goalkeepers in the history of women's soccer. She was the goalkeeper for the United States national team for most years between 1994 and 2008 and was a member of the gold-medal-winning team during the 1996 Olympic Games in Atlanta.

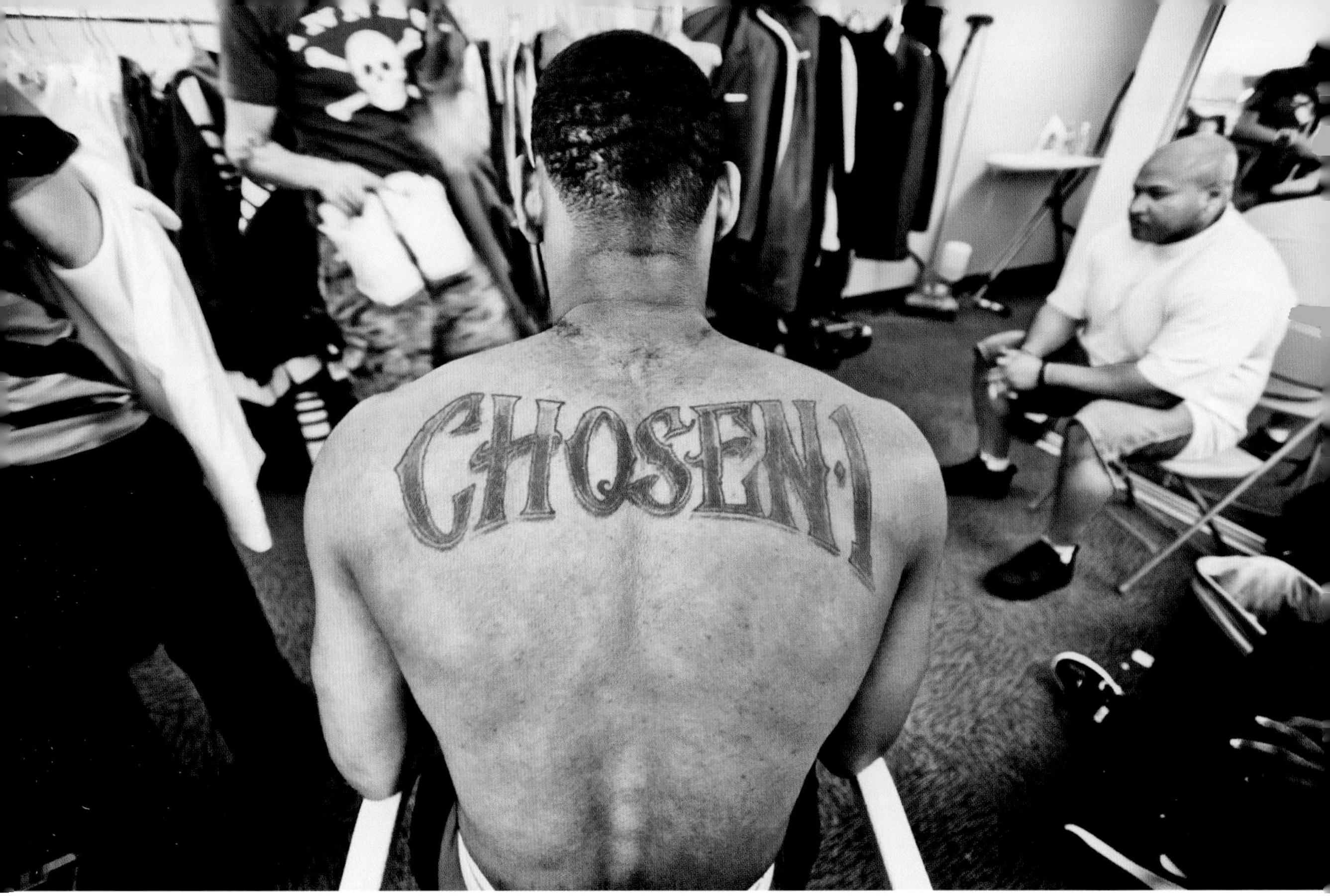

LeBron James, Cavaliers's locker room, 2005
Justin Jay
—

LeBron James, while still in high school, was already projected to become one of the greatest basketball players in NBA history.

James embraced the projections after his rookie season by having "Chosen 1" tattooed across his back.

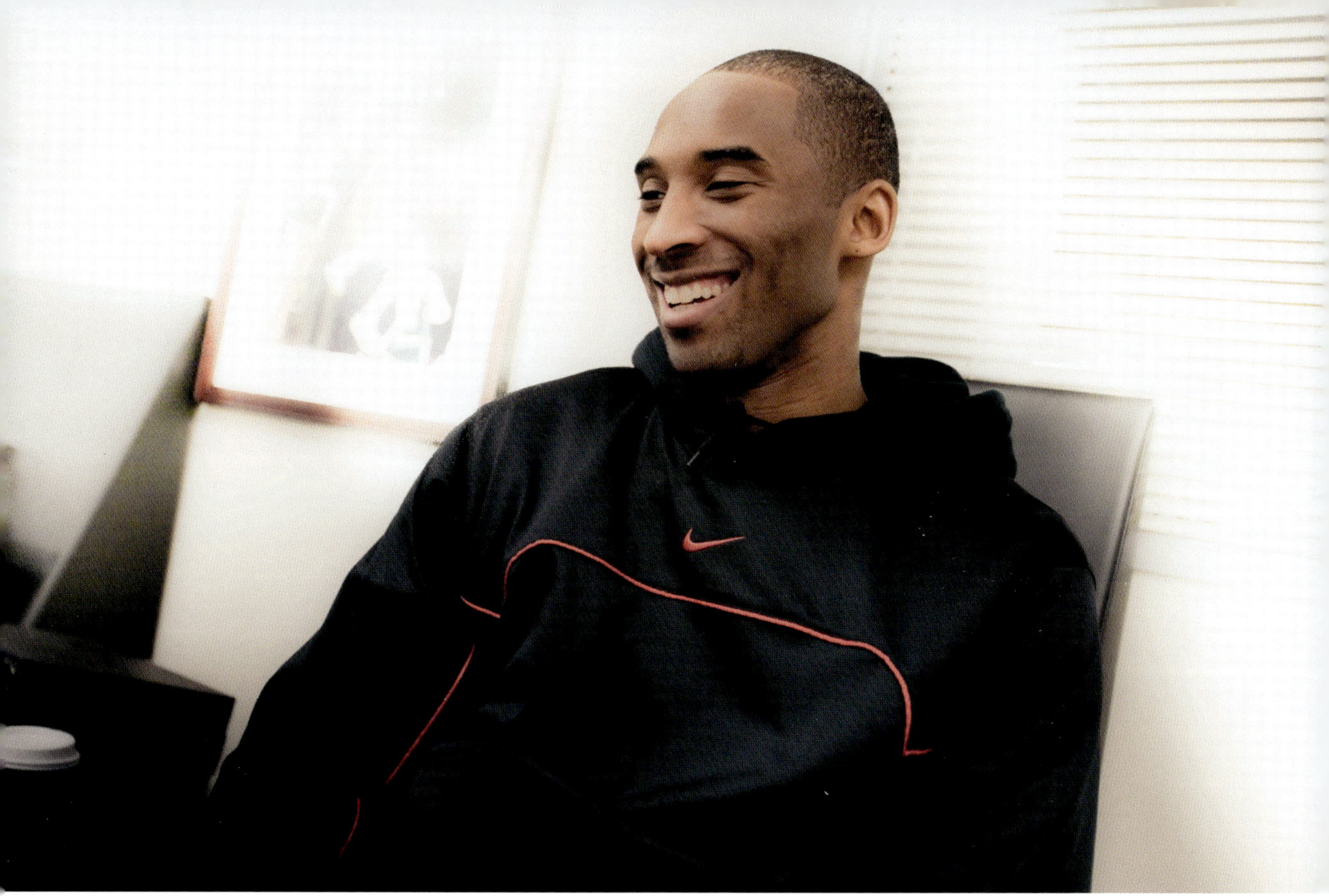

Kobe Bryant backstage at the Staples Center, 2005
Justin Jay
–

Kobe Bryant, five-time NBA champion and Hall of Fame shooting guard with the Los Angeles Lakers, adopted the nickname "Black Mamba," which reflected his obsession with being a better basketball player and a better person.

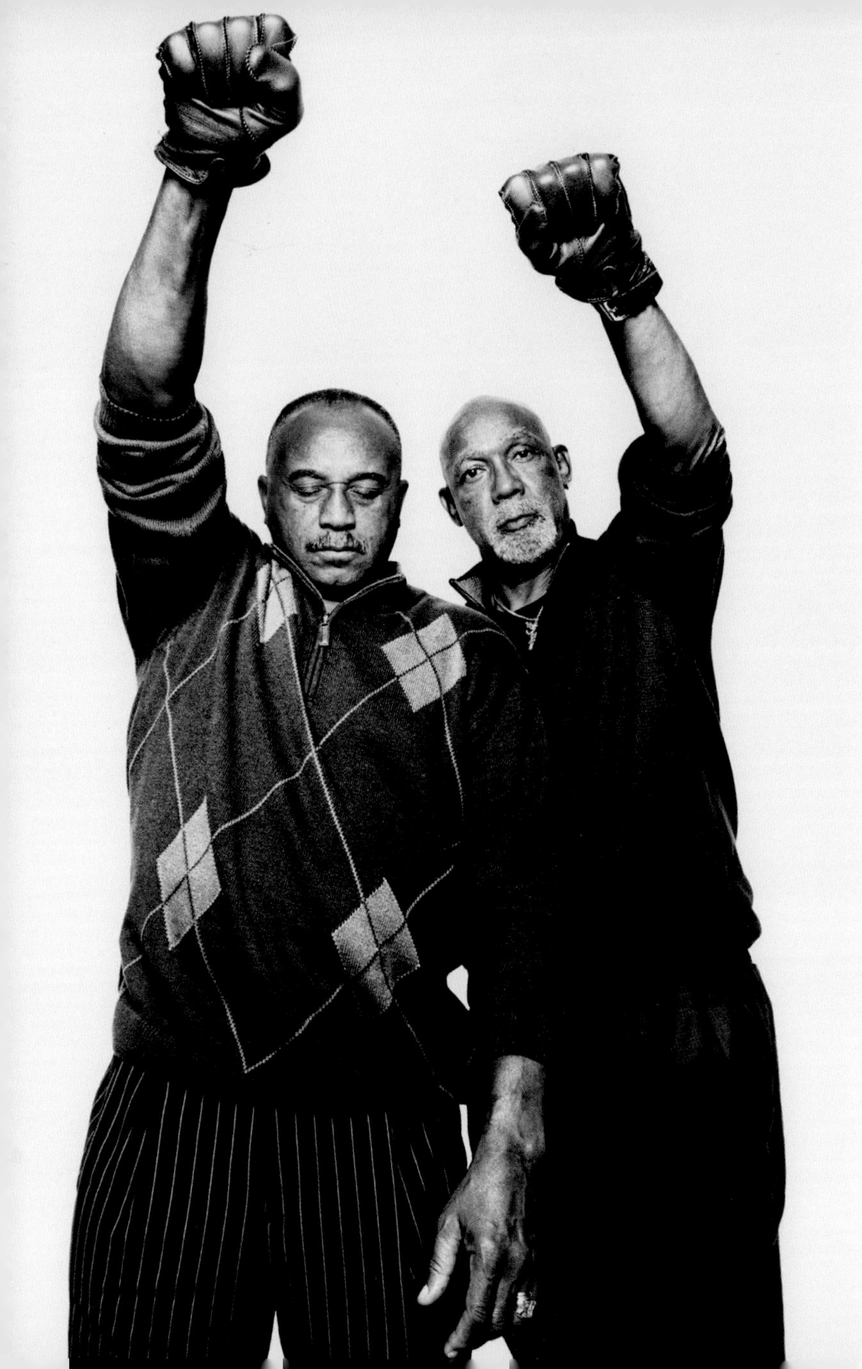

Tommie Smith and John Carlos, 2009; printed 2019
Platon

—

Olympic gold and bronze medalists Tommie Smith and John Carlos reenact their famous black-gloved, raised-fist protest from the 1968 Olympic Games in Mexico City.

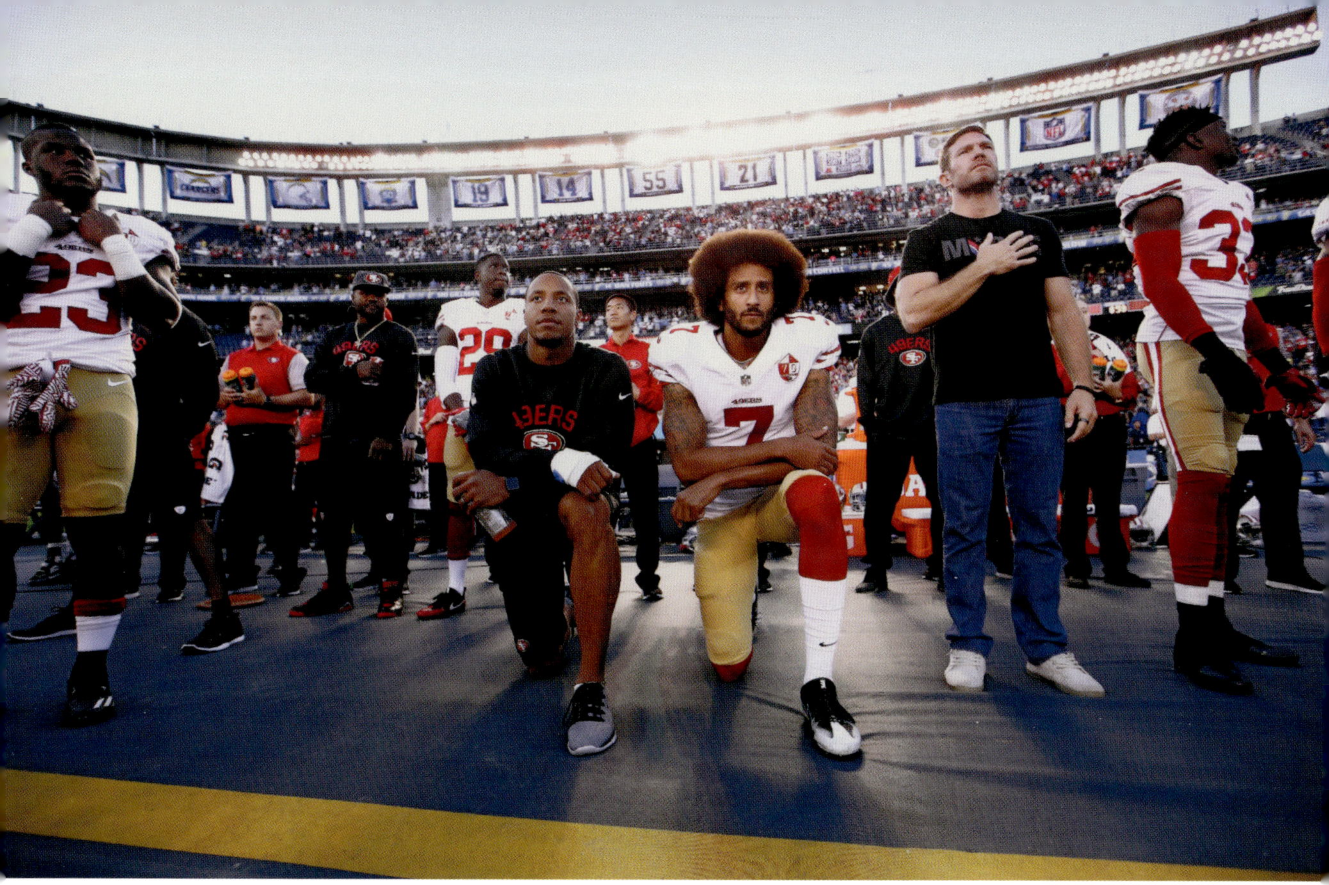

Eric Reid and Colin Kaepernick kneel during the National Anthem, San Diego, California, September 1, 2016; printed 2023
Michael Zagaris
—

Throughout the 2016 season, quarterback Colin Kaepernick took a knee during the playing of the National Anthem to protest police brutality and the unjustified killing of Black people. After a season of protesting, Kaepernick has yet to play in the NFL again.

Index

All of the photographic materials are in the collection of the National Museum of African American History and Culture.

Photographs credited "Johnson Publishing Company Archive" are jointly owned by the National Museum of African American History and Culture and J. Paul Getty Trust. Made possible by the Ford Foundation, J. Paul Getty Trust, John D. and Catherine T. MacArthur Foundation, The Andrew W. Mellon Foundation, and Smithsonian Institution.

Unidentified photographer
Ice Hockey in Harlem team and coach, after 1987
chromogenic development print
4 × 6 in. (10.2 × 15.2 cm)
Gift of Ice Hockey in Harlem
2019.74.4
© Ice Hockey in Harlem
Page 73

Unidentified photographer
Jack Johnson vs. Jess Willard, Cuba, April 5, 1915
gelatin silver print
6 3⁄8 × 9 15⁄16 in. (16.2 × 25.2 cm)
2014.3.5.1
Page 16

Unidentified photographer
New York Rens basketball game at the Renaissance Casino, November 6, 1946
gelatin silver print
10 × 8 3⁄16 in. (25.4 × 20.8 cm)
TA2020.37.2.1.4.1
Page 24

Unidentified photographer
Samuel Huston College women's basketball team, 1920s
gelatin silver print
8 1⁄16 × 10 in. (20.4 × 25.4 cm)
2014.63.109
Page 22

Unidentified photographer
A young woman with a bow and arrow, 1940s
gelatin silver print
9 5⁄16 × 7 ½ in. (23.6 × 19 cm)
2015.97.26.52
Page 21

U.S. Army
Willie Mays at Camp Kilmer, New Jersey, May 31, 1952
gelatin silver print
9 × 7 1⁄8 in. (22.9 × 18.1 cm)
TA2020.37.1.1.2.1
Page 32

George Kendall Warren
Aaron Molyneaux Hewlett, gymnasium coach at Harvard University, 1859–71
albumen print on mount
13 1⁄8 × 10 in. (33.3 × 25.4 cm)
2014.174.9
Page 20

Theodore Williams
Wilt Chamberlain and Kareem Abdul-Jabbar, 1972
color slide
Johnson Publishing Company Archive
Page 11

Ernest C. Withers
Connie Morgan, Martin Stadium, Memphis, TN, ca. 1954
gelatin silver print
13 15⁄16 × 11 in. (35.4 × 27.9 cm)
2009.16.15
© Dr. Ernest C. Withers, Sr.
courtesy of the WITHERS FAMILY TRUST
Page 31, back cover

Ernest C. Withers
Ernie Banks, Larry Doby, Matty Brescia, Jackie Robinson, Martin Stadium, Memphis, TN, 1953
gelatin silver print
16 × 20 in. (40.6 × 50.8 cm)
2009.16.14
© Dr. Ernest C. Withers, Sr.
courtesy of the WITHERS FAMILY TRUST
Page 10

Ernest C. Withers
Larry Brown with Fans, Martin Stadium, Memphis, TN, ca. 1945
gelatin silver print
11 × 14 in. (27.9 × 35.6 cm)
2009.16.12
© Dr. Ernest C. Withers, Sr.
courtesy of the WITHERS FAMILY TRUST
Page 30

Ernest C. Withers
Marcia "Toni" Stone and Unidentified Teammate, Martin Stadium, Memphis, TN, ca. 1954
gelatin silver print
11 x 14 in. (27.9 x 35.6 cm)
2009.16.16
© Dr. Ernest C. Withers, Sr.
courtesy of the WITHERS FAMILY TRUST
Page 37

Michael Zagaris
Eric Reid and Colin Kaepernick kneel during the National Anthem, San Diego, California, September 1, 2016; printed 2023
chromogenic print
16 × 20 in. (40.6 × 50.8 cm)
2024.5
© Michael Zagaris
Page 81